COMFORT FOOD THE COWBOY WAY

KENT & SHANNON ROLLINS

COMFORT FOOD
THE COWBOY WAY

BACKYARD FAVORITES, COUNTRY CLASSICS, AND STORIES FROM A RANCH COOK

HARVEST
An Imprint of WILLIAM MORROW

HarperCollins books may be purchased for educational, business, or sales promotional use. For information, please email the Special Markets Department at SPsales@harpercollins.com.

FIRST EDITION

Designed by Melissa Lotfy
Stock art: denim © olgers/Shutterstock; bandana © BOSSICA/Shutterstock

Library of Congress Cataloging-in-Publication Data has been applied for.

ISBN 978-0-358-71279-4

23 24 25 26 27   TC   10 9 8 7 6 5 4 3 2 1

CONTENTS

ACKNOWLEDGMENTS

Shannon and I are truly blessed because the folks who have helped us down this trail are salt-of-the-earth people. On ranches, we depend on a good team of horses to get us from camp to camp. With this book, we sure hitched up to a good team.

First, I would like to thank my sweet wife, Shannon, for all the hours she has endured with me, many long days and short nights. She has spent countless hours behind a camera and in front of a computer. She has made me a better cook and a much better person.

The second bunch of folks we would like to acknowledge is our extended YouTube family. We have the best fans in the world, and we are beyond honored and humbled that you let us into your homes every week. We wish we could give each one of you a hug and a thank-you for supporting our videos.

A big thank-you to our friends at Certified Angus Beef® brand. They have made me a better cook and given me a better understanding of good-quality beef, both on and off the hoof. Their generosity toward nonprofit work and education makes them a true class act.

YETI coolers have kept me out of a bind many times when cooking on remote ranches. Food storage is essential in my line of work, and these coolers have never let me down. This company's appreciation of the outdoors and dedication to making high-quality gear to withstand Mother Nature's extreme conditions have made our lives easier.

Hasty Bake stands for what we hold important, and that is quality products. Their grills, made in the USA, bring folks together to share food from the fire. We thank y'all for what you do and what you stand for.

To our book agent, Janis Donnaud, we thank you, darling, for putting up with us and making us better authors. We trust you and thank you for trusting us.

And finally, to all those old wagon cooks and cowboys who went down those dusty trails before us, we tip our hat to you.

INTRODUCTION

Comfort comes in many forms, from the clothes we wear to our surroundings and the food we eat. I think growing up we all have those memories of backyard cookouts, family reunions, and Sunday dinners. It was often a time when family traditions and recipes were served up in hearty portions. There is just something about those old classic dishes that have been passed down through the generations that do more than fill your stomach; they bring about peace and togetherness. That is what comfort food is—a sense of contentment brought on by memories of good home cooking. Comfort food is hearty dishes that have not only stood the test of time but that also rekindle a memory with every bite.

In this book, it is Shannon's and my goal to celebrate all the classic recipes that have brought us comfort through the years, whether it's Grandma's special pie, or a meal from a favorite hole-in-the-wall diner that wasn't on any tourist map, or a creation born from hard times that is still replicated today. It's important for us to remember not only these recipes but also the history and stories behind them.

Being a chuck wagon cook, my most important job is to feed cowboys. My second most important job is to make them feel comfortable in camp, to feel like family and give them a sense of being at home. When cooking on remote ranches, my home isn't made of solid walls but of canvas. The conditions are much different than a typical dining room. The chairs are replaced with wood benches, and the fine china with enameled plates. But wherever Shan and I are cooking, we want to create a sense of home and comfort, and what's the easiest way to do that? With food.

It is a special feeling when I see plates licked clean after a meal and hear the comment, "That was just like Mama used to cook." A comparison to a mama or grandma is probably the highest compliment you can get. I love cooking true homestyle foods, and not only is this a way to share food and fellowship, but it's also an opportunity to pass on traditions and history.

Cowboys need to be fed well to work well. It's very common for cowboys to lose weight during spring or fall works because the hours horseback are long, the nights short, and they're burning a lot of calories throughout the day. However, those fellers often have to let out another notch on their belts after too many extra helpings at the wagon. It's often those homestyle favorites that do it.

I've walked in the boots of some tough cooks who came before me. I admire those old men who sat in that wagon seat, driving an ornery team of mules, day after day, in some of Mother Nature's harshest conditions. Our cooking methods today are still the same, but I'm grateful for the wider selection of groceries we have to work with now. In our area, we have a great influence of Mexican cooking. This dates back to the cattle drive days, when many Mexican immigrants became cooks on the trail.

With that came the influence of new spices, including dried chiles, fresh oregano, ground cumin, among others. These spices found their way into a lot of dishes that were prepared during the long journey north. I've always said I like a dish that bites back, and we're sharing some of my favorite authentic Mexican dishes, with a little heat. The heat comes from traditional chiles that we use, whether they are ground down or rehydrated for sauces. This is what makes these recipes unique—you won't be using prepackaged seasonings, but creating a unique blend of flavors that you might only find south of the border.

Along with good Mexican food, some of my greatest memories of comfort food come from cafés and diners that populated small-town main streets, as well as one greasy spoon that served up the best patty melt in five counties. We didn't grow up with a lot of money, so café dining was sure a treat, and we looked forward to special occasions when we could indulge. I know Mama enjoyed the night off from cooking and doing the dishes!

When I was on the road doing a lot of rodeoing, I looked forward to pulling into these little diners to satisfy some hunger pains. I might be in the mood for a chili cheese dog with homemade chili or maybe a famous Oklahoma fried onion burger. These are the places where you can count on the menu being filled with all-American comfort

foods that are filling and satisfying. Now, most of the old stops I went to across rural America are boarded up and no longer exist, but we're saving you some gas money since you can now re-create these classic café dishes right at home.

Let's not forget that good outdoor cooking—which is what I'm known for. One of my favorite methods of cooking is with fire and cast iron. Now, you may not have a 385-pound wood stove like my Bertha, but you can still enjoy these flame-grilled recipes we're going to share with you. And don't you be using any briquettes! Whether it's smoking or grilling, these recipes are guaranteed to give you that authentic fire flavor with natural wood. Outdoor cooking is one of the most social types of cooking, so let's celebrate gathering around the fire!

There have been several times that I've cooked for ranches when I didn't know anyone on the crew and it was in new country. You know when you're in those situations, you often feel a little out of place. But the things that put me back in the saddle were the things that I had always relied on, and that was cooking, fire, and cowboys. It's not a good feeling being out of your comfort zone, so you have to look to something you can count on, like family, friends, your trusty roping horse, and even food. I have found out that in what may seem like the worst of times or the biggest challenges, if you just ride that horse a little longer, there ain't nothing you can't overcome.

The uncomfortable becomes comfortable, and the hopeless becomes hopeful.

The pages ahead are not just filled with feel-good recipes. We want to also take you on a journey through history. This book provides you with a ticket right in the wagon seat to travel with us to some of the ranches where we've cooked. It is filled with stories that explore what it was like going down the dusty trails in the 1800s to modern-day cowboy mischief that I seemed to get myself into growing up. This will be a look back at the tales of cooks, cowboys, and cow bosses who blazed the trails before us. If the stories don't transport you, then surely Shannon's beautiful photography will give you an up-close view into our unique lifestyle.

So get in the wagon seat—there ain't no seat belt, so just hold on tight! We're traveling to your favorite café, that authentic Mexican restaurant down the road, and the backyard to smell that good woodsmoke roll off the grill. You'll be tasting it all with a little cowboy twist, because sharing food and history has been going on around the table for centuries. It is what gets us through both times of crisis and times of celebration. It is important that we carry on these traditions and re-create comfort wherever you may hang your hat.

GOOD GRAVY!
BREAKFAST

It was a cold November night in the Palo Duro Canyon of Texas. Factor in the forty-mph winds and it sure wasn't a night for calm sleeping conditions. I remember the flapping of the canvas walls of my teepee hitting me in the head every time Mother Nature took a breath. That's one thing about Mother Nature: She's always in charge of the lighting and the thermostat when ranch cooking.

On nights like these, I'd always sleep with my clothes next to me so in the morning they'd be warm and I wouldn't have to fight putting on a stiff pair of half-frozen britches. I was afraid to look at the actual temperature when I woke up that morning, but I knew I had to stoke Bertha (my trusty wood stove) full of mesquite knots that morning to melt the layer of ice in my kitchen. I had snapped in all the walls around the fly of the wagon to help block the arctic blast, and I was determined to get my kitchen as warm as possible for those cowboys I could hear rustling in their teepees.

I knew those fellers needed all the calories they could get in order to work in these seemingly *unbearable* conditions. As a good cowboy friend of mine would always say, "This isn't a Pop-Tart kind of moment in life." He was right—this was a hearty hot biscuits and gravy morning, with lots of sausage stirred into that creamy gravy. In case you are wondering, I believe gravy is its own food group. This breakfast was an easy deal because the biscuits didn't need time to rise, so I had more time to gather firewood for Bertha.

As I combined the flour with my hands, it was hard to get my fingers moving like they should, but I knew I had to take care of this bunch because it's my job to keep them fed, no matter the conditions. I also wanted to make extra so they could stick a couple of biscuits in their pockets for a midmorning snack.

When the boys slowly started to wander into camp, they were coated in an armor of denim and wool. They all hunched over the stove with outstretched hands. Bertha doesn't have many friends in August, but in the winter, she sure is a popular ol' gal.

I said, "Grab a cup of coffee, make yourselves as comfortable as you can, and I will get all this ready to go." One of the younger cowboys leaned over to me and nearly in a whisper said, "Mr.

Rollins, how can we get comfortable? It's not fit for man nor beast to be out in this." He sure had a point. It was cozy in camp, but one inch outside those walls and my mustache hair would begin to freeze. I paused for a moment, then looked him in the eye and answered, "It may be cold and windy, but we are the lucky ones. We've got dry wood, a hot breakfast, and good friends around us. I reckon the good Lord is keeping us as comfortable as we need to be." Sometimes during the uncomfortable times in life, you just saddle up and tell yourself, *This horse may be a little* *rough to ride, but with time, things will smooth out. It's like a good skillet of gravy—if you just keep stirring, you'll get all the lumps out eventually.*

It's like a good skillet of gravy—if you just keep stirring, you'll get all the lumps out eventually.

It took many trips to the local doughnut shop, and a bigger size in britches, but we figured out how to make the perfect doughnut at home. This dough is light, airy, and deep-fried to perfection. We top it with a sweet glaze of vanilla and almond extracts, and as Shan says, "Don't forget the sprinkles!"

HOMEMADE DOUGHNUTS

MAKES 12 TO 14 DOUGHNUTS

PREP TIME: 2 HOURS AND 15 MINUTES

TOTAL TIME: 2 HOURS AND 25 MINUTES

1¼ cups milk

2 tablespoons dry yeast

½ cup plus 1 tablespoon sugar

4½ to 5 cups all-purpose flour, plus more for dusting

1 teaspoon salt

1 stick butter, softened, plus more for greasing

2 large eggs

1 teaspoon vanilla extract

Oil, for frying

Glaze (recipe follows)

1. In a small saucepan over low heat, warm the milk to room temperature. Be careful not to overheat. Pour the milk into a small bowl and whisk in the yeast and 1 tablespoon of sugar. Let the mixture rest for 10 minutes, or until bubbly.

2. Sift 4½ cups of the flour into a large bowl. Stir in the salt.

3. In a separate large bowl, using an electric mixer, cream together the remaining ½ cup sugar, the butter, eggs, and vanilla until smooth.

4. Make a well in the center of the flour mixture and pour in the yeast mixture, then the egg mixture. Slowly begin folding the ingredients together until combined. Sift in more flour, if needed, to form a soft ball that isn't too sticky.

5. Turn the dough out onto a floured surface and knead for about 8 minutes.

6. Form the dough into a ball and place in a bowl greased with butter. Cover and let rise in a warm place for about 1 hour, or until doubled in size.

7. Turn the dough out onto a floured surface and roll or pat out to ½ to ¾ inch thick. With a 3-inch biscuit cutter, cut the doughnuts out. Be careful not to twist the cutter while cutting, which can seal the edges and prevent rising.

8. With a shot glass or smaller cutter, cut the middles out. Place the doughnuts and doughnut holes on a floured pan or waxed paper and cover. Let rise in a warm place for 45 minutes to 1 hour, or until doubled in size.

9. In a large saucepan or Dutch oven, heat 3 to 4 inches of oil to 340°F.

10. Place the doughnuts, a few at a time, in the oil and fry about 1 minute each side, or until a light golden brown. Repeat with the doughnut holes.

11. Transfer the fried doughnuts to a wire rack and let cool slightly. Dip the tops of the doughnuts in the glaze and place back on the wire rack. Serve warm or at room temperature.

GLAZE

MAKES ABOUT 1 CUP

PREP TIME: 5 MINUTES

TOTAL TIME: 5 MINUTES

2 cups powdered sugar, sifted

¼ cup milk

½ teaspoon almond extract

1 teaspoon vanilla extract

Place all the ingredients together in a bowl big enough to dip the doughnuts in and whisk until smooth.

Don't waste your time at the drive-up window! We've remade the classic McDonald's breakfast to include more meat, eggs, and a tangy sauce. Instead of Canadian bacon, I want y'all to get a good thick-cut ham steak for a heartier sandwich. Our sauce has a little kick with a blend of mayonnaise, mustard, and horseradish. But please don't advertise this much because the neighbors will be wanting you to put a drive-up window in your kitchen.

HEARTY HAM AND CHEESE ENGLISH MUFFINS

MAKES 4 BREAKFAST MUFFINS

PREP TIME: 5 MINUTES
TOTAL TIME: 20 MINUTES

4 tablespoons mayonnaise

4 tablespoons mustard

3 teaspoons prepared horseradish, or more to taste

4 English muffins, split open

1 (1-pound) ham steak

8 slices cheddar cheese

8 large eggs

Salt and black pepper

4 tablespoons butter

1. In a small bowl, whisk together the mayonnaise, mustard, and horseradish.

2. Place the top of 1 muffin on the ham steak and cut around the ham to make a circle. Repeat to make a total of 4 cut ham rounds.

3. In a large cast-iron skillet over medium-high heat, cook the ham pieces for about 4 minutes per side, or until lightly charred. Just before finishing, place 1 cheese slice on top of each ham piece and heat until slightly melted.

4. Remove the ham from the skillet. Set aside and keep warm.

5. Return the skillet to medium-high heat. Butter the inside of 4 large biscuit cutters or open tin cans (such as a tuna fish can or similar). Place the cutters in the skillet and crack 2 eggs in the middle of each. Lightly scramble the eggs with a fork. Season with salt and pepper to taste.

6. Cook for about 2 minutes, or until the eggs set up a bit. Remove the cans and flip the eggs over. Continue cooking until the eggs have cooked through, about 2 more minutes.

7. Turn off the heat and top the eggs with 1 slice of cheese and let melt slightly.

8. Meanwhile, butter the insides of the English muffins and place in a separate skillet over medium-high heat to toast.

9. Spread the mayonnaise mixture on the insides of the muffins. Top the bottom muffin with 1 piece of ham and egg. Finish with the top of the English muffin. Serve immediately.

Here's a one-pot dish that will satisfy the hungriest bunch around the table. This casserole combines bacon and sausage, two types of cheese, red potatoes, and a smoked poblano chile to give it a little kick. Top with fried eggs and you will be able to climb any mountain that might come along. This is also a great camping recipe to do in a Dutch oven to keep your crew satisfied all morning.

MOUNTAIN MAN BREAKFAST

MAKES 8 HEARTY SERVINGS

PREP TIME: 20 MINUTES

TOTAL TIME: 1 HOUR AND 15 MINUTES

10 small red potatoes, peeled, or 2 pounds frozen hash browns

1 pound bacon, cut into bite-size pieces

1 pound ground breakfast pork sausage

1 white onion, chopped

1 red bell pepper, chopped

1 roasted poblano chile, chopped

Salt and black pepper

10 large eggs

1 cup shredded pepper jack cheese

1 cup shredded cheddar cheese

1. Preheat the oven to 350°F.

2. If using red potatoes, grate the potatoes into a large bowl and cover with water.

3. In a 12-inch cast-iron or other oven-safe skillet over medium-high heat, cook the bacon, stirring occasionally, until browned, about 5 minutes. Transfer to paper towels to drain. Leave about 2 tablespoons of bacon grease in the skillet and discard the rest.

4. Crumble the sausage into the skillet and cook over medium-high heat, stirring occasionally, until it begins to brown, about 5 minutes. Stir in the onion, bell pepper, and poblano.

5. If using red potatoes, drain the potatoes from the water, and pat dry with a towel. Stir the potatoes (or the frozen hash browns) into the sausage mixture and cook, stirring occasionally, until the onion, bell pepper, and poblano are tender and the sausage has browned, about

4 minutes. Season with salt and black pepper to taste.

6. Place 6 of the eggs in a medium bowl and whisk until smooth. Pour the eggs evenly over the sausage mixture. Sprinkle the bacon on top. Bake for 45 minutes, or until the eggs set up.

7. Sprinkle the cheeses evenly over the top and bake for another 2 minutes, or until melted. Crack the remaining 4 eggs on top and bake until the eggs are sunny side up, about 5 minutes. Serve warm.

> **TIP** If you don't have a large enough skillet to bake all this in, you can transfer the ingredients to a large casserole dish in step 6 and bake.

A good ol' buttery buttermilk biscuit slathered with gravy has always been a staple feeding cowboys at the wagon. This is a filling breakfast all on its own, but when you add crumbled sausage to the creamy gravy, it will keep a feller full until the next meal. The best part of this recipe is that there is no rise time for the biscuits, so they can be made on even the busiest of mornings.

OLD-FASHIONED BISCUITS AND SAUSAGE GRAVY

MAKES ABOUT 15 BISCUITS

PREP TIME: 15 MINUTES

TOTAL TIME: 30 MINUTES

Butter, for greasing

3 cups all-purpose flour, plus more for dusting

3 tablespoons sugar

1 heaping tablespoon baking powder

½ teaspoon salt

½ teaspoon cream of tartar or 2 teaspoons white vinegar

1½ sticks chilled butter, thinly sliced

1 large egg, lightly beaten

¼ cup buttermilk

Sausage Gravy (recipe follows)

1. Preheat the oven to 350°F. Lightly butter a large cast-iron skillet or baking pan.

2. In a large bowl, combine the flour, sugar, baking powder, salt, and cream of tartar. If using vinegar, mix in with the buttermilk in step 4.

3. With a pastry cutter or fork, cut the butter into the flour mixture. You don't want to cut it as fine as a cracker crumb consistency but leave some larger butter flakes.

4. In a small bowl, whisk together the egg and buttermilk. Stir the wet mixture into the flour mixture until just combined. The dough will be a little sticky.

5. Turn the dough out onto a generously floured surface. Flour your hands and knead the dough ten to fifteen times. If the dough is still tacky, knead in a little more flour to form a soft dough.

6. Pat or roll the dough out to ¾ to 1 inch thick. Cut out about fifteen 2½-inch biscuits.

7. Place the biscuits in the skillet or baking pan. Bake for 10 to 15 minutes, or until a light golden brown on top and bottom. Brush the tops with melted butter and serve immediately, topped with sausage gravy.

SAUSAGE GRAVY

MAKES ABOUT 3 CUPS

PREP TIME: 10 MINUTES

TOTAL TIME: 10 MINUTES

½ cup meat grease (sausage, bacon, or other meat)

5 tablespoons all-purpose flour

1½ to 2 cups milk, warmed

½ pound cooked ground pork breakfast sausage

Salt and black pepper

1. In a large cast-iron skillet over medium heat, heat the grease.

2. Sift in the flour and let it come to a light boil for 2 minutes, stirring and mashing down constantly with a flat spatula.

3. Slowly stir in 1½ cups of the milk and bring back to a light boil. Continue stirring and mashing with the spatula until the mixture is smooth and reaches the desired consistency, about 2 minutes. You can add more milk or warm water to thin the gravy, if needed.

4. Stir in the sausage. Season with salt and pepper to taste. Serve immediately over biscuits.

How about y'all hop in the wagon with me and we take a trip south of the border for breakfast? If cowboys have to saddle up quickly and get out for the day or if we're moving camp, Shan and I like to make a grab-and-go meal like this sandwich. The southwestern flavor comes from refried beans smothered on a toasted bagel with thick-cut bacon and green chiles. We've also substituted the bacon with some chorizo for even more flavor.

SOUTHWESTERN BAGEL SANDWICH

MAKES 2 SANDWICHES

PREP TIME: 5 MINUTES

TOTAL TIME: 25 MINUTES

8 tablespoons canned refried beans

1 heaping tablespoon mayonnaise

2 tablespoons canned diced green chiles

2 tablespoons butter

4 slices thick-cut bacon, cut in half

2 large eggs

2 bagels, toasted

2 slices pepper jack cheese

1 avocado, thinly sliced

Salsa, for topping (optional)

1. In a small saucepan over low heat, cook the beans, mayonnaise, green chiles, and 1 tablespoon of the butter for about 5 minutes, or until warmed through.

2. In a medium cast-iron skillet over medium-high heat, cook the bacon until crispy.

3. In a large cast-iron skillet over medium heat, melt the remaining 1 tablespoon butter over medium heat. Crack the eggs in the skillet and fry for about 3 minutes, until the whites begin to set up. With a spatula, break the yolks and spread around gently. Continue to cook for 1 to 2 minutes, then flip and cook for 2 more minutes, or until cooked through.

4. Spread the bottom bagels with about 2 tablespoons of the bean mixture each and top with 1 slice of pepper jack cheese, followed by the fried egg, 4 cut bacon strips, and half the avocado. Spoon salsa, if using, on top. Spread the inside of the bagel tops with 2 tablespoons of the bean mixture and place on top. Serve immediately.

This classic recipe was born from some hard times. Also known as poor man's gravy, this recipe originally only required two ingredients: coffee and meat drippings. Unlike traditional gravy, the liquid is made from brewed coffee, which gives it a robust flavor and was much cheaper than using milk or cream. Just goes to show you don't need fancy ingredients to serve up a good meal.

RED EYE GRAVY AND HAM

MAKES 4 SERVINGS

PREP TIME: 15 MINUTES

TOTAL TIME: 15 MINUTES

1 (12- to 14-ounce) ham steak

2 tablespoons bacon grease

1 tablespoon butter

2 tablespoons all-purpose flour

1 to 1½ cups brewed coffee

2 teaspoons black pepper

1. Heat a large cast-iron skillet over medium-high heat. Add the ham and cook for 4 minutes on each side, or until lightly charred. Transfer the ham to a large plate and set aside.

2. Return to the same skillet and melt the bacon grease and butter over medium-low heat. Sift in the flour and stir until smooth with a flat spatula.

3. Stir in 1 cup of the coffee, a little at a time. Bring to a boil, stirring occasionally. Sprinkle in the pepper and continue to cook for 3 to 4 minutes, until it reaches the desired consistency. Stir in more flour for a thicker consistency or add more coffee to thin it.

4. Remove from the heat and let cool slightly. Pour the gravy over the ham and serve immediately.

"Green grass and fat cows . . .
Man, we're sure living in tall cotton."

TOP 10 SIGNS YOU'RE A CHUCK WAGON COOK

1. Your kitchen is bigger than some states.
2. You have no electric bill.
3. Your patrons commute horseback.
4. Your watch has two times: daylight and dark.
5. The nearest grocery store is sixty miles away.
6. You don't have to mop the kitchen floor.
7. Your dishwasher and bathtub are one and the same.
8. Having a waterbed means your teepee leaked.
9. Days off only come at night.
10. To cook on high, you just add more wood.

Unlike using regular scrambled eggs, we are changing up the technique here so those eggs won't fall out of your quesadilla when you take a bite. Be sure to get a big enough cast-iron skillet that will hold the entire tortilla. We're also using lots of cheese and diced-up ham. This won't be a little ol' thin quesadilla, 'cause we're layering it up!

GREEN CHILE AND EGG BREAKFAST QUESADILLA

MAKES 2 QUESADILLAS

PREP TIME: 5 MINUTES
TOTAL TIME: 20 MINUTES
2 tablespoons butter
4 large eggs

Salt and black pepper
1 cup shredded mozzarella
2 (10-inch) flour tortillas
1 cup pepper jack cheese

1 (4-ounce) can diced green chiles
1 cup finely chopped ham

1. In a 10-inch cast-iron skillet over medium-low heat, melt 1 tablespoon of the butter. Swirl the butter around to evenly coat the skillet.

2. In a small bowl, whisk together 2 of the eggs and pour into the skillet. Cook for 2 to 3 minutes, until they begin to set up around the edges. Season with salt and pepper to taste, then sprinkle the eggs evenly with ½ cup of the mozzarella cheese.

3. Place 1 tortilla on top of the eggs and cheese and mash down slightly to seal the ingredients together.

4. Cook for about 3 minutes, until the eggs are cooked through and easily release from the skillet.

5. Flip the tortilla over and sprinkle ½ cup of the pepper jack cheese evenly on top. Sprinkle half the can of green chiles followed by half of the chopped ham on top.

6. Fold half of the tortilla over to meet the other side and mash slightly. Cook for 3 to 4 minutes, each side, or until golden brown. Repeat to make the second quesadilla. Slice in half and serve immediately.

The key to fluffy pancakes is the mixture of baking soda and baking powder. You'll also want to be sure to cook the pancakes over low heat to allow them to rise all the way. Carefully measure a level amount of flour to ensure the correct consistency when mixing these up. Cooking these pancakes in melted butter in a good cast-iron skillet gives them a savory flavor that blends well with the sweetness of the vanilla and honey.

THE PERFECT FLUFFY PANCAKES

MAKES ABOUT 16 PANCAKES

PREP TIME: 30 MINUTES
TOTAL TIME: 30 MINUTES

2½ cups all-purpose flour
6 tablespoons sugar

4 teaspoons baking powder
4 teaspoons baking soda
1½ cups milk
4 large eggs, beaten

¼ cup honey
2 teaspoons vanilla extract
4 tablespoons unsalted butter
Butter and maple syrup, for serving

1. In a large bowl, combine the flour, sugar, baking powder, and baking soda. Whisk in the milk, eggs, honey, and vanilla until smooth.

2. In a large cast-iron skillet over low heat, melt 1 tablespoon of butter. Swirl to coat the skillet. Working in batches, ladle quarter cups of the batter into the skillet.

3. Cook for 3 to 4 minutes, until the batter begins to bubble, then flip over. Continue to cook for another 2 to 3 minutes, until a light golden brown. Repeat with the remaining batter. Serve warm with butter and maple syrup.

egg |eg| *noun*

Anything resembling a hen's egg. *See also* cowboy eggs, cackleberry, hen fruit, rooster bullet.

Who said you shouldn't have a little whiskey in the morning? This breakfast classic just got a good shot of whiskey to add to the flavor, but don't worry, the alcohol cooks out but the flavor doesn't. The other star of the show is the French bread, cut into cubes. The secret is to let it dry out a bit by baking it in the oven, which allows it to soak up the batter better. This is much easier than frying up a bunch of French toast slices, but you still get that soft bite and slight cinnamon crunch.

FRENCH TOAST CASSEROLE

MAKES 10 SERVINGS

PREP TIME: 20 MINUTES

TOTAL TIME: 50 MINUTES

2 sticks butter, plus more for greasing

1 (16-ounce) loaf French bread

1 cup plus 2 tablespoons packed light brown sugar

¾ cup granulated sugar

8 large eggs

2 cups milk, half-and-half, or heavy cream

⅓ cup whiskey

4 teaspoons vanilla extract

4 teaspoons ground cinnamon

4 teaspoons ground nutmeg

½ cup chopped pecans (optional)

Powdered sugar, blueberries, and maple syrup, for serving (optional)

1. Preheat the oven to 375°F. Butter a 9 × 13-inch baking pan.

2. Cut the bread into 1-inch squares. Place on the prepared baking pan and bake for about 10 minutes, until it dries out.

3. Meanwhile, in a medium saucepan over medium heat, melt the butter. Whisk in 1 cup of the brown sugar and ¼ cup of the granulated sugar until smooth. Evenly pour the mixture into the bottom of the pan. Top with the bread cubes and press down slightly.

4. In a medium bowl, whisk together the eggs, milk, whiskey, the remaining ½ cup granulated sugar, vanilla, 2 teaspoons of the cinnamon, and 2 teaspoons of the nutmeg. Evenly pour the mixture over the bread cubes.

5. Bake for 20 minutes. Remove from the oven and sprinkle with the remaining 2 teaspoons cinnamon, 2 teaspoons nutmeg, 2 tablespoons brown sugar, and, if desired, the pecans. Continue baking for 8 to 10 minutes, until golden brown. Remove from the oven and let cool slightly before serving. Serve warm with powdered sugar, blueberries, and syrup, if desired.

If y'all know us, you know a cackleberry is an egg (also known as hen fruit or rooster bullet). We make these at our coffee shop, and folks sure like them for an easy breakfast on the go. It's like enjoying the flavors of an omelet in one bite. We whip together eggs and cream cheese for richness and mix with bacon (or you can use breakfast sausage if you'd like), bell pepper, green onion, and cheese. Make these the night before and simply microwave for an easy morning meal.

EASY MORNING CACKLEBERRY BITES

MAKES 10 TO 12 BITES

PREP TIME: 10 MINUTES
TOTAL TIME: 40 MINUTES

Butter, for greasing
4 slices thick-cut bacon, chopped

10 large eggs
4 ounces cream cheese, softened
2 tablespoons mayonnaise
1 teaspoon salt

2 teaspoons black pepper
½ red bell pepper, diced
1 to 2 green onions, chopped
¾ cup shredded cheddar cheese

1. Preheat the oven to 350°F. Butter a 12-cup muffin pan and set aside.

2. In a medium cast-iron skillet over medium-high heat, cook the bacon until crispy. Transfer to paper towels to drain.

3. In a large bowl, whisk together the eggs, cream cheese, mayonnaise, salt, and pepper until smooth.

4. Pour the batter into 10 to 12 muffin cups to about three-quarters full. Sprinkle the tops evenly with the bacon and about ½ tablespoon of the diced bell pepper. Evenly sprinkle with the green onion and about ½ tablespoon of the cheese. Lightly stir each bite with a toothpick.

5. Bake for about 30 minutes, or until the eggs are set and cooked through. Remove from the pan and let cool slightly before serving.

TIP These remove easier if baked in a silicone muffin pan.

I'll be honest; we had a hard time categorizing this dish. Is it a breakfast, or is it a supper meal? Even though it's in the breakfast section, you can sure enjoy this any time of the day. This recipe has been around a long time, dating back to the early Dutch settlements in the 1600s, when stewed chicken and gravy was served over waffles. Luckily, this meal, which combines the savory flavor of fried chicken with sweet and rich waffles, has come into popularity once again.

CHICKEN AND WAFFLES

MAKES 4 SERVINGS

PREP TIME: 15 MINUTES

TOTAL TIME: 25 MINUTES

2 large boneless, skinless chicken breasts

2 cups all-purpose flour

1 tablespoon cornstarch

3 teaspoons smoked paprika

3 teaspoons cayenne pepper

1 teaspoon salt

2 teaspoons black pepper

3 teaspoons baking powder

2 large eggs

1 cup buttermilk

Oil, for frying

Waffles (recipe follows)

Butter and maple syrup, for serving (optional)

1. Cut the chicken breasts in half and tenderize with a meat mallet. Set aside.

2. In a medium bowl, combine the flour, cornstarch, paprika, cayenne pepper, salt, black pepper, and 1½ teaspoon of the baking powder.

3. In a separate medium bowl, whisk together the eggs, buttermilk, and remaining 1½ teaspoons baking powder.

4. In a large saucepan or Dutch oven, heat about 3 inches of oil to 350°F.

5. Place the chicken into the wet mixture and let soak for about 5 minutes.

6. Remove the chicken from the wet mixture and let drain slightly, then dredge through the dry mixture. Repeat for a double coating. Place the chicken on a wire rack and let rest for 5 minutes.

7. Fry the chicken for 3 to 4 minutes on each side, or until the internal temperature is 165°F. Remove with tongs and transfer to a wire rack to cool slightly. Serve warm on top of waffles, with butter and maple syrup, if desired.

WAFFLES

MAKES ABOUT 4 WAFFLES

PREP TIME: 5 MINUTES

TOTAL TIME: 25 MINUTES

2 cups all-purpose flour

¾ cup sugar

4 teaspoons baking powder

2 large eggs, separated

1½ cups buttermilk, plus more as needed

2 teaspoons vanilla extract

4 tablespoons butter, melted

Butter, for greasing

1. In a medium bowl, combine the flour, sugar, and baking powder.

2. In a separate medium bowl, whisk together the egg yolks, buttermilk, vanilla, and melted butter.

3. Whisk the wet mixture into the dry mixture until smooth.

4. In a small bowl, using an electric mixer on high speed, beat the egg whites until foamy and thick. Fold the egg whites into the batter mixture until it reaches a consistency slightly thicker than pancake batter. You can add more buttermilk, if needed.

5. Heat a waffle iron and generously coat with butter. Carefully pour in about a quarter of the waffle batter, depending on the size of your iron, and cook for 4 to 5 minutes, until golden brown. Serve immediately.

TIP To crisp the waffles more, place in an oven heated to 400°F for about 2 minutes to allow the steam to release.

A GOOD START
APPETIZERS

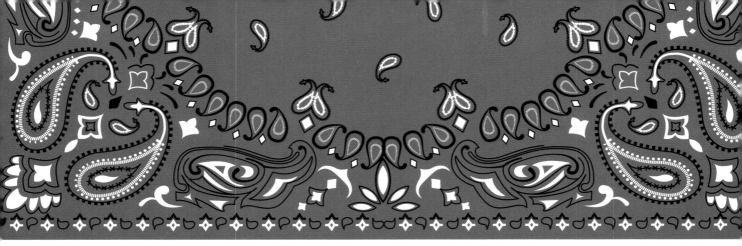

I remember when I started cooking for ranches in 1993. The first was a ranch south of Abilene, Texas, a three-week gig for spring branding. I was a little nervous, because I didn't know any of the crew . . . and they didn't know me. I wanted to make a good impression, so I figured I'd do something a little different and whip up some appetizers.

Now, back in the cattle drive days of the late 1800s, the old cook didn't have many groceries to work with. It was typically coffee, beans, flour, a little sugar, and maybe some dried meat. Also, there were only two meals a day, breakfast and supper. Even though the conditions and cooking methods are the same today, I have a lot better groceries to work with now. Since we were in Texas, I thought I'd honor the Lone Star State by making some Texas Twinkies for a starter to the meal. If y'all don't know what these are, they are a beefed-up jalapeño pepper. And when I say beefed up, I mean peppers stuffed full of good smoked brisket and cream cheese, then wrapped in bacon. I figured if anything would win those fellers over, it would be bacon!

It was a beautiful afternoon. The sky was bright blue, dotted with an occasional cloud slowly traveling above camp. It was about 3 p.m. when I started on the evening meal and fellers began showing up to check out the new cook.

You see, cowboys are just as nervous about a new cook as the new cook is. If it's a bad cook, that's three long weeks of bad food, stomach pains, and longing for a home-cooked meal. On most outfits, cowboys are known to lose weight during a works, because of the long hours on horseback, short nights for resting, and limited vittles. However, I've always prided myself on feeding those boys well enough they'll tip the scale when we all get out of there.

I started stuffing the peppers, thinking pretty highly of myself, when over my shoulder I heard one of the old-timers whisper to another, "Is this all he is fixin' for supper? We're going to starve, for sure. We may need to run this one off."

I acted like I didn't hear a thing and kept right on cooking. I dragged the grill grate out and put it on the stove to warm up as I set out the Texas Twinkies and hollered, "You fellers help yourselves!"

They frantically grabbed the Twinkies, which were gone in no time at all. You could see disappointment and some panic in their eyes—they were all thinking somebody done messed up hiring this guy as the cook! Another whisper came across camp, "Not only is he going to starve us, but we don't even get a plate."

As they began to get up and walk out of camp, I said coolly, "Hey fellers, don't be in such a hurry. We're fixin' to have supper." Still, they were hesitant as they went over to shade up under a big oak tree while I threw steaks on the grill.

When the steaks were done and I took the lid off the Dutch oven full of cobbler, the aroma guided them all back into camp. There was silence during supper, which is always a sign that I had done good. When they finished eating, they dropped their dishes in the wreck pan on the stove. As one of the older cowboys dropped his dish in the soapy water, he looked up at me and said, "Cookie, you sure had us worried when we saw you offer

them peppers. We're used to eating more than just veggies." I laughed and told him we called them appetizers—the starter of the meal until the real thing comes along.

"Oh," he said, "the only starters we knew anything about was starting a colt to make a good cow horse. Most the time those colts are contrary, and you ain't sure what they're going to do. I guess it's sorta like that meal. You gotta wait till the end to see if you got off to a good start."

> "Hey fellers, don't be in such a hurry. We're fixin' to have supper."

Have you ever had the problem where you stick your hand in a tater chip sack and it's empty? Well, we have remedied that situation, because nothing beats that flavor of a homemade potato chip. The main thing you have to have in a chip is crispness. We're sharing tips on the correct potato to use, how to blanch it for crispness, and some seasoning suggestions too.

BEST HOMEMADE POTATO CHIPS

MAKES 8 TO 10 SERVINGS

PREP TIME: 1 HOUR

TOTAL TIME: 1 HOUR AND 30 MINUTES

4 medium russet potatoes, peeled

Ice water

1 tablespoon white vinegar

Oil, for frying

Seasoning mixes (see page 29 for suggestions)

1. Rinse the potatoes well. Using a mandoline or cheese slicer, slice the potatoes thinly and place in a large bowl. Cover with ice water and let soak for 30 minutes.

2. Drain the water from the potatoes. Add more water to the potatoes and stir around to rinse. Drain the water and repeat. Continue rinsing until the water is clear.

3. In a large saucepan over medium heat, bring 4 cups water and the vinegar to a simmer.

4. Add the potatoes in small batches, and simmer for 3 minutes to blanch (the potatoes will turn from an opaque white to a clearer white). Drain the potatoes in a colander, then transfer to a cloth towel. Lightly pat to dry. Repeat with the remaining potatoes.

5. In a large saucepan or Dutch oven, heat about 3 inches of oil to 375ºF.

6. Working in batches, carefully add the potatoes, a few at a time, to the hot oil. Fry for 3 to 4 minutes, flipping occasionally, until golden brown and crispy. Remove the potatoes with a slotted spoon and transfer to a wire rack or paper towels to drain. Repeat with the remaining potatoes. Season with salt or our suggested seasonings. Let cool completely before serving.

TIP The chips can be stored in a sealed paper sack for a few days.

SEASONING SUGGESTIONS

GARLIC: 2 teaspoons garlic powder and 2 teaspoons onion salt

RANCH: 1 (1-ounce) package ranch seasoning mix and sea salt to taste

CHILI: 2 teaspoons chili powder, 2 teaspoons smoked paprika, 1 teaspoon onion salt, and 1 teaspoon dry mustard

DILL: Dried dill and sea salt, both to taste

I know a queso dip is all about the cheese, but we're kicking it up a few notches with some smoke flavor and chopped chuck roast. Velveeta is the base ingredient for a smooth and creamy dip, but we're also throwing in Monterey Jack, mozzarella, and queso fresco cheeses 'cause we don't want to be guilty of not having enough cheese! You can add any type of wood you like for flavor, but we do like a mix of mesquite, cherrywood, and/or alderwood (see Top Tips for Grilling on page 181).

SMOKED QUESO DIP

MAKES 15 TO 20 SERVINGS

PREP TIME: 2 HOURS

TOTAL TIME: 6 HOURS AND 35 MINUTES

Lime juice

1 (2- to 3-pound) chuck roast

1½ tablespoons salt

2 tablespoons black pepper

2 poblano chiles

2 jalapeños

1 pound Monterey Jack cheese, cubed

1 pound mozzarella cheese, cubed

8 ounces Velveeta cheese, cubed

1 (10-ounce) can diced tomatoes with green chiles, drained

1 cup beef broth or chicken broth

1 cup crumbled queso fresco

1. Generously rub lime juice all over the roast, then season with salt and pepper. Cover and place in the fridge for at least 2 hours.

2. Clean and oil the grill or smoker. Light hardwood or hardwood lump charcoal and heat to 225°F.

3. Place the roast on the smoker, close the lid, and smoke for about 4 hours, or until fork tender. Remove from the smoker and roughly chop. Set aside.

4. Increase the heat to 350°F. Add 1 handful of mesquite wood chips and 1 handful of applewood for flavor.

5. Place the poblanos and jalapeños on the smoker and cook until blistered, rotating occasionally. Place the chiles in a plastic bag with 1 tablespoon water and let steam for about

5 minutes. Remove the chiles from the bag, peel off the skins, and discard. Chop the chiles.

6. Place the cubed cheeses in a 12-inch Dutch oven or foil pan. Stir in the meat, peppers, and diced tomatoes with the green chiles. Pour in the broth.

7. Place the Dutch oven, uncovered, on the smoker and close the smoker's lid. Cook, stirring occasionally, for about 30 minutes. Top with queso fresco and serve warm.

> **TIP** The chuck roast can be made in a slow cooker on high for 4 to 5 hours. You also can bake the dish, stirring occasionally, in a conventional oven at 350°F until melted and bubbling, about 40 minutes.

These may be a holiday staple for some folks, but we are dishing them up year-round as an appetizer or even a side dish. This is an easy recipe to throw together with Bisquick, two types of cheese, and cream cheese to make it rich and creamy. And you know it wouldn't be cowboy cooking unless we threw in a little grated jalapeño too.

CHEESY SAUSAGE BALLS

MAKES 18 TO 20 SAUSAGE BALLS

PREP TIME: 10 MINUTES

TOTAL TIME: 35 MINUTES

1 pound ground breakfast pork sausage

8 ounces pepper jack cheese, shredded

8 ounces cheddar cheese, shredded

4 ounces cream cheese, softened

½ cup chopped green onion

1 jalapeño, shredded

2 garlic cloves, minced

1 tablespoon Worcestershire sauce

Salt and black pepper

1½ cups Bisquick mix

1. Preheat the oven to 350°F. Line a large baking sheet with parchment paper.

2. In a large bowl, use your hands to mix together the sausage, shredded cheeses, and cream cheese until well incorporated.

3. Stir in the green onion, jalapeño, garlic, and Worcestershire sauce and season with salt and pepper. Using your hands, slowly mix in the Bisquick.

4. Pinch off about 20 golf ball–size balls and place on the prepared baking sheet.

5. Bake for 20 to 25 minutes, until golden brown and set. Serve warm.

Okay, folks, if you had to pick only one recipe to cook from our appetizer chapter, this is the one! It also includes two of my favorite words: *fried* and *cheese*. We are mixing up a traditional macaroni and cheese and tossing in green chiles and bacon. To make these little fellers extra crispy, we are using a panko bread crumb coating and frying them up to a perfect golden brown.

FRIED MAC AND CHEESE BALLS

MAKES ABOUT 20 BALLS

PREP TIME: 2 HOURS AND 25 MINUTES
TOTAL TIME: 2 HOURS AND 40 MINUTES

6 slices thick-cut bacon, diced
½ white onion, diced
Salt
½ tablespoon olive oil

8 ounces uncooked large elbow macaroni
1 pound Velveeta cheese, cubed
4 tablespoons butter
4 ounces cream cheese, softened
¼ cup half-and-half

2 (4-ounce) cans diced green chiles, drained
Black pepper
2 large eggs, beaten
1 (16-ounce) box panko bread crumbs
Oil, for frying

1. In a large cast-iron skillet over medium-high heat, cook the bacon, stirring occasionally, until it begins to brown, about 4 minutes. Add the onion and cook for another 2 to 3 minutes, stirring occasionally. Remove the bacon and onion from the skillet with a slotted spoon and transfer to paper towels to drain.

2. Bring a medium pot of salted water to a boil over high heat. Add the olive oil and macaroni and cook the pasta until it just begins to soften. Be sure not to overcook. Drain the macaroni in a colander and return it to the pot.

3. Stir in the Velveeta, butter, cream cheese, half-and-half, green chiles, and bacon and onion mixture. Cook for 4 to 5 minutes, until everything is blended well and begins to simmer. Season with salt and pepper to taste.

4. Remove the pot from the heat and let cool to room temperature. Place the macaroni in a

large container, cover, and place in the fridge to completely chill, about 2 hours.

5. Place the eggs in a small bowl. Place the panko in a medium bowl.

6. Spoon out the macaroni and form into about 18 to 20 golf ball–size balls. Dip the balls in the egg, then roll in the panko to generously coat. Press the crumbs firmly to the ball with your hands to ensure they stick well.

7. In a large saucepan or Dutch oven, heat about 3 inches of oil to 350°F.

8. Working in batches, carefully add the macaroni balls, a few at a time, to the hot oil and fry until golden brown, 3 to 4 minutes. Remove with a slotted spoon and transfer to a wire rack to cool slightly and drain. Repeat with the remaining macaroni balls. Serve warm.

THE CHUCK WAGON

The chuck wagon was an absolute necessity during the cattle drive era. There had to be a cook, one who could drive the wagon, as mobility was key. A chuck wagon sure could take a beating during a thousand-mile trip up the trail.

Traveling as many as twelve to fourteen miles a day, it was safe to say that the cook spent more time in the wagon seat than he did in the bedroll. Any wagon could become a chuck wagon by taking the rear grain boards out and adding a

chuck box. Each chuck box was a little different, with drawers and shelves to meet the cook's needs.

Some wagons also pulled a smaller one-axled wagon behind. This additional wagon, called a hoodlum (hood) wagon or pup wagon, would carry extra wood, a wood-burning stove, bedrolls, and supplies. One thing is for sure: Wagons, cooks, and cowboys all had an important job, and the good ones were tough and dependable.

Chuck Box: The design of shelves and drawers that make up the cook's kitchen. Common dry goods, spices, and cooking utensils are stored here.

Chuck Box Lid: A fold-down lid from the chuck box that creates the workspace and kitchen counter.

Boot: A box secured under the chuck box to hold additional cooking equipment, such as pots, pans, and Dutch ovens.

Opossum Belly: Used to hold wood for cooking. It's typically made from cowhide that stretches and secures under the chuck wagon. Often, cow pies were collected and stored here to burn farther down the trail if wood was scarce.

Water Barrel: Ranging in size but typically holding about 30 gallons of water. On the trail drives, this barrel would be reloaded at river crossings. Today, we also use a supplementary tank and refill from that. I ration 250 gallons of water for cooking and dishes for three weeks for a crew of twelve cowboys.

Side Boxes: The boxes for holding equipment needed to work on the wagon, such as lanterns and assorted tools.

Wagon Seat: A seat known to be very uncomfortable during long drives. A cook or cowboy would often trade out the chuck wagon seat for a rolled-up bedroll for more cushioning while driving.

Tools: Any variety of useful tools including a crosscut saw, axe, sledge hammer, shovel, pickaxe, and shotgun (for hunting and incoming attacks).

Brake System: A locking brake handle along with a foot pedal located on the right hand of the wagon near the seat. The brake pads were often made of rawhide that pressed against the back wheels.

Wheels/Hubs: Mainly made of oak or ash. Sometimes a spare would be carried but mostly only the parts were carried, including spokes, hub band, felloes (outside circular part of the wheel), and steel plates. Rough ground and rocks were common enemies of the wheel and would break a spoke. Not greasing the hubs often enough also was a common error that caused wheel issues.

Block and Tackle: A device made of rope and pulleys that was used to help pull a load onto the wagon. It could also be anchored to a tree to help pull the wagon out of a deep hole.

Tongue: A 4-inch-wide by 14-foot-long piece of oak or ash, which hitched onto the front of the wagon. A team of mules or horses would be hitched to it to pull the wagon.

When it comes to picking out an onion for this recipe, pay attention to its shape. It is best to have a wide, symmetrical side where the root of the onion is because that will allow the onion to stay on its side while frying and prevent it from rolling around in the oil. This breading has a hint of Tex-Mex flavor, with a blend of ancho and traditional chili powders and a zesty dipping sauce. Be sure to separate the petals of the onion because this will help create that blossom effect and make this deep-fried dish really open up and bloom!

ONION BLOSSOM

MAKES 1 ONION BLOSSOM

PREP TIME: 15 MINUTES

TOTAL TIME: 25 MINUTES

1 cup milk

1 large egg

1 cup all-purpose flour

½ tablespoon cornstarch, plus more for sprinkling

3 teaspoons seasoned salt

3 teaspoons coarsely ground black pepper

3 teaspoons ancho chile powder

2 teaspoons garlic powder

2 teaspoons chili powder

1 teaspoon ground cumin

1 large yellow onion, preferably Vidalia or Texas Sweet

Oil, for frying

Dipping Sauce (recipe follows)

1. In a large bowl, whisk together the milk and egg.

2. In a separate large bowl, combine the flour, cornstarch, seasoned salt, pepper, ancho chile powder, garlic powder, chili powder, and cumin.

3. Cut a small flat spot on the root end (do not cut the end that has the green sprout growing from it) to make it set level. Peel the skin from the onion and place the uncut side up. With a sharp knife, make a downward slice, about ½ inch from the root end. Rotate the onion about a quarter turn and repeat the slice until you have 4 slices. Then go back and slice in between the quarter cuts to make a total of 8 slices. With your hands, spread the cut onion slices apart to resemble a bloom.

4. Sprinkle the onion lightly with cornstarch. Separate the petals while sprinkling to ensure the cornstarch coats everywhere. Place the onion in the flour mixture to coat well. Be sure to spread the onion slices apart to get it all covered well.

5. Dip the onion in the milk and egg mixture to generously coat. Shake off the excess wet mixture from the onion and place it back in the flour mixture to coat well. Shake off the excess flour and place the onion on a wire rack.

6. Add enough oil to a large saucepan or Dutch oven so that the onion can be submerged and heat to 375°F.

Recipe continues ➤

7. Carefully add the onion to the hot oil and fry for 5 to 7 minutes, until a deep golden brown and crispy. Make sure the onion is covered with oil to ensure an equal fry time on all parts.

8. Remove the onion with a slotted spoon and transfer to a wire rack to drain and cool slightly. Serve warm with dipping sauce.

DIPPING SAUCE

MAKES ABOUT ¾ CUP

PREP TIME: 5 MINUTES
TOTAL TIME: 30 MINUTES

½ cup mayonnaise
2 tablespoons prepared horseradish

1 tablespoon ketchup
1 tablespoon Worcestershire sauce
½ tablespoon spicy brown mustard
1 teaspoon smoked paprika

1 teaspoon coarsely ground black pepper
1 teaspoon garlic powder

In a medium bowl, whisk together all the ingredients. Cover and place in the fridge for at least 30 minutes before serving.

Let's be honest, it's hard to beat good ol' bacon. But have you heard the saying "Like a kid in a candy store"? Well, here we are. Be sure to start with thick-cut bacon, the thicker the better. This is marinated in jalapeños and Worcestershire sauce, then coated with brown sugar, garlic powder, onion powder, and cinnamon for a sweet and savory combination. Use this in sandwiches, as a salad topping, or as a snack.

CANDIED JALAPEÑO BACON

MAKES 6 TO 8 SERVINGS

PREP TIME: 55 MINUTES

TOTAL TIME: 1 HOUR AND 10 MINUTES

2 jalapeños, stemmed, seeded, and diced

2 tablespoons Worcestershire sauce

1 pound thick-cut bacon, separated into slices

1 cup packed light brown sugar

2 teaspoons onion powder

2 teaspoons garlic powder

1 teaspoon ground cinnamon

Coarsely ground black pepper

1. In a large bowl, mix together the jalapeños and Worcestershire sauce. Add the bacon and toss to coat well. Cover and refrigerate for at least 30 minutes.

2. Meanwhile, in a small bowl, combine the brown sugar, onion powder, garlic powder, and cinnamon.

3. Remove the bacon from the bowl and shake off some of the jalapeños. Note: The more peppers left on, the spicier the bacon. Place the bacon on a wire rack on top of a baking sheet covered with foil.

4. Sprinkle the bacon generously with the brown sugar mixture. Season with black pepper. Pat the mixture into the bacon. Flip the bacon and repeat on the opposite side. Let rest for 15 minutes.

5. Preheat the oven to 375°F.

6. Bake for about 25 minutes, or until your desired doneness. Serve warm or at room temperature.

TIP When completely cooled and dry, the bacon can be stored in an airtight container for up to 5 days in the fridge.

I had a lot of requests on our YouTube channel to try and re-create the iconic McDonald's French fry. This took me over a year to figure out! McDonald's uses about eighty-five different ingredients in their fries (not really, but it's a lot), but we are simplifying things. One trick is rinsing and drying the fries well before soaking them in beef broth. You also are going to fry these twice in a mixture of oil and lard for maximum crispness.

CRISPIEST FRENCH FRIES

MAKES 4 SERVINGS

PREP TIME: 2 HOURS AND 10 MINUTES
TOTAL TIME: 2 HOURS AND 30 MINUTES

6 cups ice water, plus more for rinsing

½ cup sugar

2 teaspoons vinegar

2 tablespoons salt

2 (1-ounce) packets beef bouillon powder

2 russet potatoes, peeled

Oil, for frying

1 cup lard

Sea salt

1. In a large bowl or pot, combine the ice water, sugar, vinegar, salt, and 1 packet of the beef bouillon. Set aside.

2. Cut the potatoes into thin, even strips. Rinse the potatoes in a colander well with ice water. Repeat.

3. Submerge the fries in the ice water and sugar mixture. Cover and place in the fridge for 2 hours.

4. Drain the fries in a colander, then transfer to paper towels. Scatter the fries out and dry well with the paper towels.

5. Pour 2 to 3 inches of oil in a large saucepan or Dutch oven and heat to 300°F.

6. Working in batches, carefully add the fries, a few at a time, to the hot oil and fry for 5 minutes. Remove with a slotted spoon and transfer to paper towels to drain. Repeat with the remaining fries.

7. Add the lard to the oil and increase the temperature to 415°F. When the lard has melted, add the fries a batch at a time. Fry for 1 to 2 minutes, or until crispy and a light golden brown. Remove with a slotted spoon and transfer to clean paper towels to drain. Immediately sprinkle with salt to taste. Serve warm.

This is an easy recipe, and it will sure impress the neighbors when you pull this off your smoker. Harder cheeses, like cheddar, tend to smoke a little better because they don't melt as easily, but you can use nearly any cheese you like. To prevent the cheese from melting too quickly, I recommend freezing the cheese first, then smoking it in cooler outdoor temperatures (see Tip). Remember, not too much heat is required; you just want good smoke, so keep that in mind when adding wood to your smoker (see Top Tips for Grilling on page 181).

SMOKED CHEESE

MAKES ABOUT 4 SERVINGS

PREP TIME: 45 MINUTES
TOTAL TIME: 3 HOURS AND 45 MINUTES

8 ounces cheese of your choice (see headnote)

Ice

1. Freeze the cheese for about 30 minutes before smoking.

2. Soak a few handfuls of hardwood chips in water for about 45 minutes before smoking. You can use any flavor you like, but I prefer mellower-flavored woods, including fruit- or oakwoods.

3. Meanwhile, add a heaping handful of hardwood chunks or hardwood lump charcoal in a small pan or tin plate. Light the wood on fire and wait until it's ashy white before starting.

4. Set the plate at the farthest point from the grill grates as you can on your smoker or grill and to one side for indirect heat. Add the soaked wood chips to the plate. Make sure all the vents are wide open to create good smoke.

5. Fill an aluminum pan with ice and place a wire rack on top. Place the cheese on the rack. Place the pan on the indirect heat side of the grill (farthest from the heat) and close the lid. Cook for 1 hour. Check the ice at about 30 minutes to see if it needs to be replenished.

6. Flip the cheese over and add more soaked wood chips for additional smoke. Continue smoking for 1 to 1½ hours for softer cheeses, or 1½ to 2 hours for harder cheeses. Be sure to check the ice and smoke levels about every 20 minutes. Drain the water and replenish ice as needed.

7. Remove the cheese from the smoker and let cool. Place in a plastic bag and set in the fridge for at least 6 hours or up to overnight. The longer it sets, the more smoke flavor will absorb.

TIP I do recommend smoking cheese in cooler outdoor temperatures. If cooking when it's warmer outside, you may need to reduce your smoking time to prevent the cheese from melting.

Have you been looking for a good chicken wing recipe? Instead of the typical Buffalo-style chicken wing, we're changing it up with a garlicky Parmesan coating and a hint of smoke and heat. Baking them in a light flour coating is what gives these wings a crispy finish. Whether it's game day or an evening in the backyard, these will be a crowd pleaser.

GARLIC PARMESAN CHICKEN WINGS

MAKES ABOUT 6 SERVINGS

PREP TIME: 20 MINUTES

TOTAL TIME: 50 MINUTES

3 pounds chicken wings

½ cup all-purpose flour

4 teaspoons dry mustard

4 teaspoons garlic powder

4 teaspoons smoked paprika

1 tablespoon ancho chile powder

½ tablespoon seasoned salt

½ tablespoon coarsely ground black pepper

½ cup hot sauce

3 tablespoons Worcestershire sauce

2 teaspoons liquid smoke

½ cup minced garlic

¾ cup grated Parmesan cheese

1. Preheat the oven to 400°F.

2. Dry the wings well with paper towels and set on a wire rack.

3. In a large bowl, mix together the flour, dry mustard, garlic powder, paprika, ancho chile powder, seasoned salt, and pepper.

4. In a large bowl, combine the hot sauce, Worcestershire sauce, and liquid smoke.

5. Toss the chicken wings in the wet mixture and let them soak for at least 10 minutes. Shake off any excess.

6. Generously coat the wings, one at a time, in the flour mixture, then place on a wire rack for at least 5 minutes to dry.

7. Place the rack on a large baking sheet and place in the oven for about 20 minutes. Spoon the garlic on the wings and continue cooking for 10 minutes, until golden brown. Remove from the oven and sprinkle generously with the Parmesan cheese. Serve warm.

After you make this and take a bite—or a few—you'll wonder why we didn't put this in the main course section of the book. This is a full-meal deal, not just beans and some cheese sauce. With its layers of southwestern seasoned beef, jalapeños, pinto and black beans, and a homemade sour cream drizzle, we just hope your chips can handle all the goodness!

SUPREME NACHOS

MAKES 12 TO 15 SERVINGS

PREP TIME: 15 MINUTES
TOTAL TIME: 25 MINUTES

1 large bag tortilla chips
1½ pounds 80% lean ground beef
1 tablespoon chili powder
2 teaspoons dried oregano
2 teaspoons ground cumin
2 teaspoons smoked paprika
Salt and black pepper

1 (15-ounce) can black beans, drained and rinsed
1 (15-ounce) can pinto beans, drained and rinsed
2 garlic cloves, minced
8 ounces Velveeta cheese, cubed
1 tablespoon butter
⅓ cup heavy cream
½ teaspoon liquid smoke

3 teaspoons red pepper flakes
¾ cup sour cream
½ cup pickled sliced jalapeños with juice, plus more for topping
1 tablespoon honey
2 cups shredded cheddar cheese
2 cups shredded Monterey Jack cheese
1 small white onion, chopped, for topping

1. Preheat the oven to 375°F.

2. Spread the chips on a large rimmed baking sheet and place in the oven for about 15 minutes.

3. Meanwhile, in a large cast-iron skillet over medium-high heat, cook the ground beef until browned, stirring occasionally, about 5 minutes. Drain the grease and discard. Return the beef to the skillet.

4. Stir in the chili powder, oregano, cumin, and paprika. Season with salt and black pepper to taste. Stir in the black beans, pinto beans, and garlic. Simmer over medium-low heat for about 5 minutes, stirring occasionally.

5. Place the Velveeta cheese in a small saucepan over low heat. Stir in the butter and cream. Cook for 4 to 5 minutes, stirring until smooth. Stir in

the liquid smoke and 1 teaspoon of the red pepper flakes. Cook on low heat, stirring occasionally, for about 2 minutes.

6. In a medium bowl, combine the sour cream, pickled jalapeños, the remaining 2 teaspoons red pepper flakes, and the honey. Add a little of the jalapeño juice until the mixture reaches a pourable consistency.

7. Remove the chips from the oven. Sprinkle about a third of the shredded cheeses evenly on the top, followed by a third of the meat mixture, a third of the cheese sauce, and a generous drizzling of the sour cream mixture. Repeat until all the ingredients have been used. Top with the onion and, if desired, additional jalapeños. Serve immediately.

This recipe is a popular dish here in this part of the country. Don't worry, no armadillos are harmed in the making of this recipe. The eggs are actually deep-fried jalapeños, stuffed with cream cheese and wrapped in sausage. Potato flakes make up the crust for a good crunch.

ARMADILLO EGGS

MAKES 12 POPPERS

PREP TIME: 15 MINUTES

TOTAL TIME: 30 MINUTES

12 jalapeños

6 to 8 ounces cream cheese, softened

½ cup shredded cheddar cheese

2 teaspoons garlic, minced

2 teaspoons onion powder

1½ pounds ground breakfast pork sausage

3 large eggs

2 cups instant potato flakes

Oil, for frying

Jalapeño Popper Sauce, for serving (page 51)

1. With a small knife, cut out a narrow opening from the top of each jalapeño to the bottom and remove the seeds. Keep the stems attached.

2. Roast the peppers over a burner until they just begin to blister and soften.

3. In a small bowl, combine the cream cheese, cheddar cheese, garlic, and onion powder. Evenly stuff the jalapeños with the cheese mixture.

4. Divide the sausage into 12 equal pieces. Take 1 sausage slice and roll it out thinly between two pieces of waxed paper.

5. Place a jalapeño in the center of the sausage and form the sausage around the pepper, leaving the stem poking out. Repeat with the remaining jalapeños and sausage.

6. In a small bowl, beat the eggs. Pour the potato flakes into a separate small bowl. Roll the wrapped jalapeños in the eggs, then generously coat with the potato flakes. Dip the jalapeños back in the eggs and again in the potato flakes for a double coating.

7. In a large saucepan or Dutch oven, heat about 3 inches of oil to 350°F.

8. Working in batches, carefully add the jalapeños, a few at a time, to the hot oil and fry for about 4 minutes, or until they are a deep golden brown and crispy. Remove with a slotted spoon and transfer to paper towels or a wire rack to drain and cool slightly. Repeat with the remaining jalapeños. Serve warm with dipping sauce, if desired.

This style of popper is nearly a full meal since the jalapeños are packed full of barbecue brisket and cream cheese, then wrapped in thick-cut bacon. Try it with our Smoked Brisket with Burnt Ends (page 185) or our Apple-Smoked Pulled Pork (page 223), though you can substitute any type of meat here. These Twinkies will go fast, so make a double batch and don't forget the honey and ranch dipping sauce.

TEXAS TWINKIES

MAKES 12 POPPERS

PREP TIME: 10 MINUTES
TOTAL TIME: 40 MINUTES

12 jalapeños
1 cup chopped brisket

2 tablespoons barbecue sauce, or to taste
6 to 8 ounces cream cheese, softened
2 teaspoons onion powder

2 teaspoons minced roasted garlic
12 slices thick-cut bacon
Jalapeño Popper Sauce, for serving (recipe follows)

1. Preheat the oven to 400°F.

2. With a small knife, cut out a long and narrow slit from the top of each jalapeño to remove the seeds. Keep the stems attached.

3. In a medium bowl, combine the brisket, barbecue sauce, cream cheese, onion powder, and garlic.

4. Stuff the jalapeños with the brisket mixture. Wrap each jalapeño with 1 slice of the bacon and secure with a toothpick.

5. Place a wire rack on top of a cookie sheet and arrange the jalapeños on top of the rack. Bake for 25 to 30 minutes, or until the bacon is crispy and the jalapeños have softened. Allow the jalapeños to cool slightly before serving. Serve with dipping sauce, if desired.

> **TIP** If you prefer crispier bacon, cook the bacon about halfway before wrapping around the jalapeños.

JALAPEÑO POPPER SAUCE

MAKES ABOUT ¾ CUP

PREP TIME: 5 MINUTES
TOTAL TIME: 35 MINUTES

½ cup honey
1 (1-ounce) package ranch seasoning mix

3 teaspoons Worcestershire sauce
3 teaspoons prepared horseradish

In a small bowl, whisk together all the ingredients until smooth. Cover and place in the fridge for at least 30 minutes before serving.

BELOW THE RIM

Long before the dawning,
Not a creature heard about.
Old bones they start to aching,
As tired muscles begin to shout.
He struggles from his bedroll,
Tired and broke and bent.
Mornings they come early below the rim,
When you're under ol' Cookie's tent.
This country called the Palo Duro,
Rough country, wild and free.
Jagged rocks on canyon rims,
Deep draws full of mesquite trees.
An old black hat sets on his head,
Weathered by sweat and smoke.
As he kneels there on the ground,
The morning fire he begins to stoke.
It is a battle to stand upright,

And he is proud to make it once more.
His once strong muscles have faded,
Like time washes sand from the shore.
Sixty years he's been a wagon cook,
And time it hasn't been too fair.
Weathered, scared, and weary,
He has seen and done his share.
They say he broke his back,
I believe it was in the fall of '83.
A runaway team flipped the wagon,
And it was the next day before they got him free.
I heard a big grizzly once came into his camp.
He was on the prowl and looking for a fight.
But that old cook shot every shell he had,
Then every man enjoyed a good stew that night.

. . .

There are many wrinkles on his face,
Etched there by time and sun.
Maybe they're a message or reminder,
That his race is nearly done.
You will never hear him say much,
But I'd give anything to know his story.
Oh, you'll catch a little mumble every now
    and then,
Something about his days of glory.
They say he came over from England,
A young'un of fourteen, a stowaway on a boat.
He craved the cowboy lifestyle,
From reading dime novels, some feller wrote.
You can ask him about his past,
He'll just say it sure went by in a flash.
Then he'll go back to making biscuits,
Stirring gravy and making hash.

His eyes still have a little sparkle,
But like his lantern they too are growing dim.
His gait is somewhat slower,
As the first hint of morning peeks above the rim.
But you won't catch him loafing,
His food is always hot.
The grub it is aplenty,
And coffee is always in the pot.
You won't find his name in any history book.
Or a plaque of him on any wall.
But to me he was a living legend,
Though bent, no other man would ever stand as tall.

. . .

Many suns have set and years gone by,
But I will never forget my time with him,
Or the stories he shared or the memories made,
On those mornings there below the rim.

A PLACE TO HANG YOUR HAT
HOMESTYLE COMFORT FOOD

Cowboy hats are sort of like a good pair of boots. The longer you wear them, the better they feel, but sometimes they need a little help feeling just right. I have had hats that needed a little shimming with a paper towel to help get the right snugness so it will stay on in a forty-mph breeze. Over time, an abundance of sweat and smoke will have it molded to your melon just right.

The cowboy hat comes in many different shapes and styles, and some are a reflection of the region. A tight crease of the brim up the sides, often called a taco crease, can be found in South Texas. A shorter crown in the shape of a *D* can be spotted in the West and Central Texas regions, as well as the New Mexico area. A flat brim and shorter crown, also known as the Buckaroo crease, is common in the Great Basin area and travels north into Montana. The traditional cattlemen's crease is the most common and is found nationwide. And once in a while, you'll still see the Monty Walsh, the old Hollywood style with a tall, pronounced crown and large brim. Straw hats are worn in the hotter weather and felt hats in the cooler months. And even though there are many different styles, my dad always told me, "Don't judge a man by the shape of his hat or the horse he rides—it's what's in his heart that matters."

The cowboy helmet, as I've heard it called so many times, always comes off at mealtime. Whether it's in a house or in camp, the rules are the same. In camp, those cowboys typically place them crown side down beside a stool or between the legs under a bench. It's a sign not just of reverence but also respect. There may not have been a proper door to enter my kitchen on the prairie, but those fellers knew the unwritten code. Just as if each one were dining with me at home, them hats would come off just after that threshold was crossed.

A comfortable hat is important to a feller, and so is having a comfortable place to hang your hat. It's something I take serious at the wagon, because I want folks to be comfortable in my camp. To make folks feel comfortable, there are two things that need to happen: You make them food they want to eat, and you make them feel welcome where the food is served. Ranch cooking has taught me a lot of lessons, not all of them about fire and iron and cooking but about life lessons as well. Treat folks like you want to be treated and feed folks from the heart. Your plates will always be full, and guests will always grace your table.

We've all heard the saying "Home is where you hang your hat." My hats have hung in teepees, wagon seats, and tree branches. And my homes haven't all been brick and mortar. They have been portable, made of canvas and rope, staked to the ground to withstand the hardships of Mother Nature's fury. But comfort comes in many forms and fashions. My tables were of tin and weathered wood, and more times than not, they were graced with a covering of dust rather than a fine linen tablecloth. But what was on the table were heaping helpings of comfort food, hearty dishes that filled your heart and soul. My goal has always been to create meals that bring you back to a special place, a special time. There's no telling how many times I've heard someone on a crew say as he dropped a plate in the wreck pan, "My mother used to cook something like that" or "Last time I ate this was at my grandmother's house." These are the recipes that have been handed down through many generations and were born of family gatherings. They are recipes that often have memories attached.

So no matter what hat you wear in life, wear it with pride. And wherever you hang your hat at the end of the day, whether it's in a big-city apartment or on eighty acres, we hope your hat and your home bring you shelter and comfort.

> "Treat folks like you want to be treated and feed folks from the heart."

I think we all grew up on Hamburger Helper or some variation of it. However, instead of using the box, let's do this homemade-style and get some great flavors going. This is a budget-friendly one-pot meal that will feed a crew. Ground beef, green chiles, cream cheese, sour cream, and cheddar combine for a generous helping of creamy, cheesy goodness. For extra flavor, go ahead and substitute the cheddar cheese for our Smoked Cheese (page 44).

ONE-POT CREAMY BEEF AND MACARONI

MAKES ABOUT 6 SERVINGS

PREP TIME: 5 MINUTES
TOTAL TIME: 25 MINUTES

2 pounds 80% lean ground beef
2 cups uncooked large elbow macaroni

2 cups beef broth
1 large white onion, diced
4 garlic cloves, minced
1 to 2 (4-ounce) cans chopped green chiles

½ cup sour cream
4 ounces cream cheese, softened
2 cups shredded cheddar cheese
Salt and black pepper

1. In a large cast-iron skillet or pot over medium-high heat, cook the ground beef until browned, stirring occasionally, about 5 minutes. Drain the grease and discard. Return the beef to the skillet.

2. Stir in the macaroni, broth, onion, garlic, and green chiles.

3. Cover and bring to a simmer for about 12 minutes, or until the macaroni is tender.

4. Remove the skillet from the heat and stir in the sour cream and cream cheese until smooth.

5. Place the skillet over low heat and stir in the cheddar cheese. Cook, stirring occasionally, until the cheese has melted. Season with salt and pepper. Serve warm.

"All things considered, getting bucked off wasn't near as bad as hitting the ground."

A shepherd's pie and cottage pie are very similar with one difference: the meat. A shepherd's pie is traditionally made with lamb, while the cottage pie uses beef. So, since this is a cowboy cookbook, can you guess what my favorite is? Shredding the veggies is the trick to get this pie to hold its shape when slicing, and the whipped potatoes mixed with eggs, cream, and Parmesan give this a fluffy and unique crust topping.

COTTAGE PIE WITH PARMESAN POTATOES

MAKES ABOUT 6 SERVINGS

PREP TIME: 20 MINUTES

TOTAL TIME: 50 MINUTES

4 russet potatoes, peeled

1 pound 80% lean ground beef

2 teaspoons salt

2 teaspoons black pepper

2 medium carrots, grated

2 celery stalks, grated

1 yellow onion, grated

2 tablespoons tomato paste

$\frac{1}{2}$ cup beef broth

2 tablespoons dry red wine

1 tablespoon Worcestershire sauce

1 tablespoon minced garlic

1 cup frozen corn

2 large egg yolks, beaten

$\frac{1}{3}$ cup heavy cream

2 teaspoons garlic powder

1 cup shredded Parmesan cheese, plus more for topping

All-purpose flour for thickening, if needed

1. Position a rack in the middle of the oven and preheat the oven to 400°F.

2. Cut the potatoes into large, even chunks and place in a large pot. Cover with water and bring to a boil until tender, about 10 minutes. Drain well.

3. Meanwhile, in a large cast-iron skillet over medium-high heat, cook the ground beef until browned, stirring occasionally, about 5 minutes. Drain the grease and discard. Return the beef to the skillet and season with salt and pepper.

4. Reduce the heat to medium and stir in the carrots, celery, and onion. Stir in the tomato paste and broth until smooth. Cook for about 5 minutes, stirring occasionally.

5. Stir in the wine, Worcestershire sauce, garlic, and corn. Cook a few minutes to warm through.

6. In a large bowl, mash the potatoes until smooth. Stir in the egg yolks, cream, garlic powder, and Parmesan cheese. Season with salt and pepper. Be sure the potatoes are stiff enough to stay on the spoon. If they are too moist, add a little flour to thicken.

7. Keep the beef mixture in the skillet or transfer to a 9 × 13-inch baking dish and top with the mashed potatoes. With a fork, lightly press into the potatoes and pull up to create slight peaks around the top. Sprinkle evenly with additional Parmesan cheese.

8. Bake for 20 to 25 minutes, until the top is lightly browned and the potatoes set up and form a sponge-like crust. Let rest for about 5 minutes before serving.

A hearty noodle recipe is actually a staple for me to make when cooking for ranches on a cold day. I need something that is warm and comforting and will fill a feller's belly. I like to use a chuck roast, but you could also substitute with a strip steak or sirloin. A splash of white wine deglazes the pan and adds a light, fruity flavor to the creamy mushroom sauce. Use a wide egg noodle for a richer pasta flavor that will bond to the sauce better.

BEEF STROGANOFF

MAKES 6 TO 8 SERVINGS

PREP TIME: 25 MINUTES
TOTAL TIME: 1 HOUR AND 10 MINUTES

2½ pounds chuck roast

Coarsely ground salt and black pepper

4 tablespoons butter

½ cup dry white wine

1 medium yellow onion, thinly sliced

6 cloves garlic, minced

1 pound white button or cremini mushrooms, stemmed and sliced

1½ cups beef broth

1 tablespoon Worcestershire sauce

¼ cup all-purpose flour

12 ounces uncooked wide egg noodles

1 cup sour cream

Chopped green onions, for serving (optional)

1. Cut the beef against the grain into about ½-inch-wide by 1½-inch-long strips.

2. In a large bowl, generously season the meat strips with salt and pepper.

3. In a large cast-iron skillet over medium-high heat, melt 2 tablespoons of the butter. Add half of the beef to the skillet and cook for about 2 minutes to sear. Flip the steak over, and cook an additional 2 minutes. Transfer the beef to a medium bowl and set aside. Melt 1 tablespoon of the butter and repeat with the remaining beef.

4. Add the wine to deglaze the skillet. Be sure to scrape the brown bits off the bottom of the pan with a wooden spoon or spatula. Scrape all the contents of the skillet into the bowl with the beef.

5. Return the skillet to the heat and melt the remaining 1 tablespoon butter. Add the onion and cook, stirring occasionally, for about 3 minutes.

Add the garlic and mushrooms and cook, stirring occasionally, until the onion and mushrooms are soft, about 5 minutes.

6. Whisk in the broth, Worcestershire sauce, and flour until smooth. Return the beef to the skillet, cover, and cook over medium-low heat, stirring occasionally, until the beef is tender, about 40 minutes.

7. Meanwhile, cook the noodles according to the package directions. Drain well, return to the pot, and lightly coat with additional butter or olive oil. Keep warm.

8. Stir the sour cream into the beef mixture and let simmer for about 2 minutes, stirring frequently. Taste and adjust seasoning as needed.

9. Spoon the beef mixture over egg noodles and, if desired, top with chopped green onions.

On Saturday afternoons, Grandma and I would watch Cajun chef Justin Wilson on PBS. I loved to hear him talk and tell his stories. He was my introduction to Cajun food. I first cooked this dish in Louisiana for a bull sale many years ago. At the time, I didn't have a clue about grits or a roux. But, folks, when you can combine the Holy Trinity of Cajun cooking with a good browned roux . . . everyone is going to want to be from down south! Adding cheese to the grits gives them a more rounded flavor and makes these grits the perfect vehicle to pile on the shrimp. As Justin Wilson said, "I gaaar-un-tee you going to like dis."

SHRIMP AND GRITS

MAKES ABOUT 4 SERVINGS

PREP TIME: 5 MINUTES

TOTAL TIME: 45 MINUTES

2 teaspoons salt

1 cup coarse-ground white grits (not instant)

2 cups half-and-half

2 pounds raw shrimp, peeled and deveined

Juice of 1 lemon

1 dried ancho chile, crushed, or ½ tablespoon ancho chile powder

8 slices thick-cut bacon

½ cup chopped celery

1 red bell pepper, chopped

1 yellow bell pepper, chopped

1 white onion, chopped

1 (4-ounce) can diced green chiles

2 garlic cloves, minced

4 tablespoons butter

¼ to ⅓ cup all-purpose flour

1 cup chicken broth

1 tablespoon Worcestershire sauce

1 to 1½ cups shredded cheddar or sharp cheddar cheese

1. Pour 3 cups water into a large saucepan, add the salt, and bring to a boil. Whisk in the grits and half-and-half. Reduce the heat to a simmer and cover. Continue cooking, stirring occasionally, until the grits have thickened and are tender, 15 to 20 minutes. Set aside and keep warm. As the grits set, they will thicken up more. Be sure the grits aren't too runny before serving.

2. Meanwhile, place the shrimp in a small bowl and toss in the lemon juice and ancho chile until coated. Set aside and let marinate until ready to use.

3. In a large cast-iron skillet over medium-high heat, cook the bacon, stirring occasionally, until browned, about 5 minutes. Transfer to paper towels to drain. Leave the bacon grease in the skillet. When cooled, chop the bacon.

4. Return the skillet to the heat and stir in the celery, bell peppers, and onion. Cook, stirring occasionally, until the onion is tender, about 5 minutes.

5. Stir in the green chiles, garlic, and shrimp. Turn off the heat and set aside.

6. In a small saucepan over medium heat, melt the butter. Whisk in ¼ cup flour and continue whisking to create a smooth roux. Reduce the heat to low and cook, stirring constantly, until the mixture is a golden brown color and nearly as thick as a paste, about 8 minutes. Add more flour, if needed, to achieve the desired consistency. Watch carefully, as the mixture can burn easily.

7. Place the skillet with the shrimp over medium heat and stir in the roux. Stir in the broth, Worcestershire sauce, and bacon. Cook, stirring occasionally, until the sauce thickens up and the shrimp turns opaque white with some pink, about 8 minutes.

8. Meanwhile, add the cheese into the warm grits and stir until melted. Divide the grits among four plates and evenly top with the shrimp mixture. Serve immediately.

THE FRUGAL COWBOY MEAL

This ain't no Hardee's,
Nor is it a Mickey D's.
There ain't no drive-up window,
And a menu you won't see.
This is just an old chuck wagon,
That's been to hell and back.
And you won't see no Happy Meal,
'Cause my food don't come in a sack.
We don't give no little toys,
With the meal that you receive.
But we'll pass out the Rolaids,
They're about the only thing that's free.
We don't have no pretty waitress,
To bring out your gourmet meal.
Just an old, wore-out camp cook
That's nasty, mean, and ill.

'Cause he's been up early fixin' your meal,
It didn't come precooked.
And there ain't no telling what fell in it,
When you weren't there to look.
But his coffee is always hot and black,
You won't find no preservatives here.
And the meat is 100% pure,
Mostly coyote, opossum, and deer.
Now don't get all squeamish,
We ain't killed nobody yet.
And with each meal you'll receive a coupon,
For a free visit to the vet.
So get up in line here, folks,
For a frugal cowboy meal,
Before Cookie gets to tenderizing it,
With them big ol' wagon wheels.

This is an inexpensive dish that graced our table many a supper growing up. Simple ingredients are transformed by creating a homemade sauce of cream, chicken broth, garlic, and lots of cheese. Top this off with a Ritz cracker crust, 'cause as Andy Griffith always said, "Everything's better with a Ritz!"

TUNA CASSEROLE WITH PARMESAN CRACKER CRUST

MAKES 6 TO 8 SERVINGS

PREP TIME: 15 MINUTES

TOTAL TIME: 35 MINUTES

12 ounces uncooked egg noodles

3 tablespoons butter

1 white onion, diced

4 garlic cloves, minced

4 tablespoons all-purpose flour

2 cups chicken broth

1 cup heavy cream

4 (6-ounce) cans white albacore tuna in water, drained

1 cup shredded cheddar cheese

1 cup shredded Monterey Jack cheese

1½ cups crushed Ritz crackers

½ cup grated Parmesan cheese, plus more for sprinkling

2 tablespoons avocado oil or olive oil

1. Preheat the oven to 400°F. Lightly grease a 9 × 13-inch casserole dish or 12-inch cast-iron skillet.

2. Cook the noodles according to the package directions.

3. Meanwhile, in a large pot over medium heat, melt the butter. Stir in the onion and cook until softened, about 5 minutes.

4. Stir in the garlic and flour and cook for 1 minute, stirring constantly. Slowly stir in the broth and cream. Bring to a simmer for about 3 minutes, or until the mixture thickens slightly, stirring frequently.

5. Stir in the tuna, cheddar, and Monterey Jack.

6. When the pasta is done, drain, then fold it into the cheese sauce until well coated. Pour the mixture into the prepared casserole dish.

7. In a small bowl, combine the cracker crumbs, Parmesan cheese, and oil. Evenly sprinkle the mixture over the pasta.

8. Bake for 20 minutes, or until the bread crumbs are lightly browned and the casserole is bubbling through. Sprinkle with additional Parmesan cheese and serve warm.

Are y'all ready to wok and roll? This cooks up great in a wok, but you can break out a large cast-iron skillet, if you prefer. This is a great summertime meal to throw together with fresh garden veggies, like squash, taters, and bell peppers. We're tossing it all up in a beer and mustard sauce that coats the meat well and creates a savory glaze. We're using bratwurst, but you can easily substitute chicken, beef, chorizo, and so on. Serve this over rice for a full meal.

BRATWURST AND BEER STIR-FRY

MAKES 6 SERVINGS

PREP TIME: 10 MINUTES

TOTAL TIME: 35 MINUTES

4 tablespoons avocado oil

1 (19-ounce) package bratwurst, cut into 1-inch pieces

3 large red potatoes, roughly chopped

2 yellow summer squash, sliced

1 red bell pepper, cored and sliced

1 green bell pepper, cored and sliced

2 small white onions, sliced

2 garlic cloves, minced

3 tablespoons honey mustard

6 ounces light beer

2 tablespoons Worcestershire sauce

Salt and black pepper

Chopped green onions, for topping

1. In a wok or large cast-iron skillet over medium-high heat, heat the avocado oil. Add the bratwurst and cook, stirring occasionally, until browned and lightly crisped, about 5 minutes. Move the sausage up the walls of the wok (if using a skillet, remove but keep warm).

2. Add the potatoes and cook until about three-quarters done, about 5 minutes. Push to the top of the wok (or remove) and add the squash. Cook, stirring occasionally, until they start to become tender, 2 to 3 minutes. Move the squash up the walls or remove.

3. Add the bell peppers and onions and cook until tender, stirring occasionally, about 3 to 4 minutes.

4. Stir the potatoes, sausage, and squash together with the bell peppers and onions. Stir in the garlic and cook, stirring occasionally, for about 3 minutes.

5. Meanwhile, in a small bowl, whisk together the honey mustard, beer, and Worcestershire sauce. Pour the sauce into the meat mixture. Reduce the heat to medium-low and cook, stirring occasionally, for just a few minutes until the sauce reduces slightly.

6. Season with salt and pepper to taste. Top with green onions and serve warm.

> **TIP** Lemon-lime soda can be substituted for beer.

This is one of my favorite cuts of beef and often called "the king of the steakhouse." This is a big ol' boy that is meant to be shared and has a rich beefy flavor with its combination of marbling and tenderness. You've got to do this in a cast-iron skillet for the best sear to lock in all that flavor. The herb butter, with its blend of fresh garlic, rosemary, and thyme, is just icing on the cake . . . or steak.

PORTERHOUSE STEAK
WITH HERB BUTTER

MAKES 2 SERVINGS

PREP TIME: 2 HOURS

TOTAL TIME: 2 HOURS AND 15 MINUTES

1 (28-ounce) Porterhouse steak

Juice of 1 lime

Salt and black pepper

Coarsely ground black pepper, for coating

1 stick unsalted butter, softened

2 garlic cloves, minced

1 tablespoon minced fresh rosemary

1 tablespoon minced fresh thyme

1 tablespoon minced green onion

½ tablespoon finely crushed dried ancho chile or 1 teaspoon ancho chile powder, or more to taste

1 tablespoon butter

2 tablespoons avocado oil or olive oil

1 pound white button or cremini mushrooms, stemmed and sliced

1. Rub both sides of the steak with lime juice and generously season with salt and pepper.

2. Coat the outside edges with coarsely ground pepper. Cover the steak and place in the fridge for 1 hour.

3. Remove the steak from the fridge and let come to room temperature, about 1 hour.

4. In a medium bowl, mash the softened stick of butter. Stir in the garlic, rosemary, thyme, green onion, and ancho chile.

5. Spoon the butter mixture on a piece of plastic wrap and form into a log. Cover with the wrap and place in the fridge for 1 hour to chill.

6. In a large cast-iron skillet over medium-high heat, melt the butter with the oil. When the mixture begins to brown, add the steak to the skillet. Cook for 4 minutes on each side.

7. Flip the steak over and place 2 tablespoons of the herb butter in the skillet and 1 tablespoon on top of the steak. Cook for 2 minutes, frequently basting the steak with the melted butter.

8. Flip the steak over, place 1 tablespoon of the herb butter in the skillet and 1 tablespoon on top of the steak. Cook for 2 minutes, basting frequently.

9. Transfer the steak to a large plate and let rest for about 5 minutes. Leave the butter in the skillet.

10. Meanwhile, place the skillet over medium heat. Add the mushrooms and cook, stirring occasionally, until slightly softened, about 4 minutes. You can add more herbed butter while cooking, if needed. Serve the steak warm topped with mushrooms.

TIP   Leftover herbed butter can be used for spreading over bread or bagels or stirred in mashed potatoes.

I always figured this recipe was a secret and complicated dish with lots of ingredients. Surprisingly, this is one of the easiest pasta dishes you could prepare. Traditionally, it only has butter and Parmesan cheese, but we're making this dish a little richer by adding cream and Romano cheese for even more Italian flair. Feel free to add grilled chicken to this recipe to make it a little heartier.

FETTUCINE ALFREDO

MAKES 8 SERVINGS

PREP TIME: 5 MINUTES

TOTAL TIME: 20 MINUTES

1 pound uncooked fettucine

2 teaspoons salt

2 sticks butter

3 garlic cloves, minced

¾ cup heavy cream

¾ cup shredded Parmesan cheese, plus more for sprinkling

¾ cup shredded Romano cheese, plus more for sprinkling

Coarsely ground black pepper, for topping

Smoked paprika, for topping (optional)

Chopped fresh parsley, for topping (optional)

1. In a large pot, add the pasta and cover with water. Stir in the salt and bring to a boil over high heat. Cook according to the package instructions. Reserve about 1 cup of the pasta water, drain the pasta, and return to the pot to keep warm.

2. Meanwhile, in a large cast-iron skillet over medium heat, melt the butter. Stir in the garlic and cook for 1 to 2 minutes. Stir in the cream. Cook for about 5 minutes, stirring frequently while the cream reduces.

3. Add the Parmesan and Romano cheeses and stir until melted. If the sauce is too thick to pour, thin it slightly with some of the reserved pasta water.

4. Pour the sauce over the pasta and toss to coat. Sprinkle with additional cheeses and top with some coarse grindings of pepper, and, if using, paprika and chopped parsley. Serve immediately.

"Manners don't cost a thing, but the impression of rudeness can be very costly."

Over the years, this dish has had many names: Sh@% on a Shingle, Save Our Stomachs, Save Our Souls, and the Same Old Stuff. It appears the first published recipe was an army version from the early 1900s that called for chipped beef and evaporated milk. It also became a staple during the Depression as an inexpensive meal that could be made with any dried meat, a little flour, milk or water, and toast. We're still keeping with tradition but making this a little more palatable by using ground beef, a rich and creamy gravy, and serving it over a thick garlic toast.

S.O.S.

MAKES 4 SERVINGS

PREP TIME: 5 MINUTES

TOTAL TIME: 15 MINUTES

1 pound 80% lean ground beef

½ yellow onion, chopped

Salt and black pepper

5 tablespoons butter

4 tablespoons all-purpose flour

2 cups milk, plus more as needed

4 slices thick-cut bread or garlic bread, toasted

1. In a large cast-iron skillet over medium-high heat, cook the beef, stirring occasionally, until it begins to brown, about 4 minutes. Stir in the onion and continue cooking until the beef has browned and the onion is tender, another minute or so. Drain the grease and discard. Return the beef and onion mixture to the skillet and season with salt and pepper to taste.

2. In a medium skillet over medium heat, melt the butter. Stir in the flour with a flat spatula until smooth. Slowly pour in the milk. Continue cooking and stirring until the mixture thickens to a gravy, 3 to 4 minutes. Season with salt and pepper to taste.

3. Pour the gravy mixture into the beef skillet. Stir for 2 to 3 minutes until well incorporated. Add more milk to thin the mixture, if needed.

4. Evenly spoon the mixture over the toast and serve immediately.

Even though I've worked with cows all my life, I'm a big fan of fish, and salmon is a great one to sear up. This recipe combines a lemon butter sauce with cherry tomatoes, all cooked up in a cast-iron skillet to make this a one-skillet dish. To achieve the perfect cook on the salmon, gently press down on the fillet with a fork. If the flesh flakes or separates easily, the fish is done. Serve it with some rice or even noodles to round out the meal.

LEMON BUTTER SEARED SALMON WITH CHERRY TOMATOES

MAKES 2 SERVINGS

PREP TIME: 30 MINUTES
TOTAL TIME: 45 MINUTES

2 (6-ounce) salmon fillets, skin on
Sea salt and coarsely ground black pepper

1½ tablespoons avocado oil or olive oil
4 tablespoons butter
2 garlic cloves
Leaves from 1 sprig fresh thyme, roughly chopped

Leaves from 1 sprig fresh rosemary
12 cherry tomatoes, halved
1 tablespoon capers, drained
Juice of ½ lemon

1. Take the fillets out of the fridge and let sit about 30 minutes to warm up. Pat dry with paper towels.

2. With a knife, make ½-inch-deep scores about ½ inch apart on the flesh side of the salmon. Be careful not to cut all the way through.

3. Spread the slices apart slightly and sprinkle with salt and pepper. Turn the fish over and season again.

4. In a large cast-iron skillet over high heat, heat the oil. When it just begins to smoke, reduce the heat to medium and place the fillets, skin side down, in the skillet. Press the fillets down slightly with a spatula. Cook for about 3 minutes to sear.

5. Flip the fillets over, reduce the heat to medium-low, and add 2 tablespoons of the butter, the garlic cloves, thyme, and rosemary.

6. When the butter melts, tilt the skillet and spoon the butter mixture over the top of the fillets. Let the fish cook for about 3 minutes, basting frequently.

7. Flip the fillets to skin side down and move to one side of the skillet. On the opposite side of the skillet, add the tomatoes and the remaining 2 tablespoons of butter. Stir in the capers.

8. Drizzle the lemon juice on the tomatoes and salmon and cook for about 3 minutes, stirring the tomatoes frequently, until the tomatoes soften slightly and the fillets' flesh is flaky.

9. Place the salmon on two plates and spoon the tomatoes, capers, and butter sauce evenly over both. Serve immediately.

Now don't get to thinking this isn't authentic—we just added a cowboy twist to it. I made a very important call to my good Italian friend, Joe Parlanti. Even though he has a secret family recipe that he couldn't share, he did give me some pointers and must-haves in an authentic lasagna. It's all about the sauce! Be sure you give this plenty of time to cook, because the longer it cooks, the better the flavor. I'm also tossing in some green chiles and jalapeño for a little cowboy inspiration. Don't let the long list of ingredients scare you—it's simple and just takes a little time.

THICK AND ZESTY LASAGNA

MAKES ABOUT 8 SERVINGS

PREP TIME: 3 HOURS AND 15 MINUTES
TOTAL TIME: 4 HOURS AND 15 MINUTES

12 Roma tomatoes
½ cup chopped fresh parsley
¾ cup chopped fresh basil
½ cup chopped spinach
12 garlic cloves
2 white onions, chopped
1 (10-ounce) can diced tomatoes and green chiles, drained
2 tablespoons Italian seasoning

2 teaspoons salt
2 teaspoons black pepper
4 tablespoons extra-virgin olive oil
1 tablespoon Worcestershire sauce
1½ pounds ground beef
1 pound sweet Italian sausage
1 pound white button or cremini mushrooms, stemmed and chopped
1 teaspoon fennel seeds
½ teaspoon red pepper flakes, plus more for topping

4 tablespoons butter
1 (8-ounce) can tomato paste
½ cup dry red wine
2 pounds ricotta cheese
2 cups diced mozzarella cheese
4 cups shredded mozzarella cheese
½ cup minced fresh parsley
⅓ cup grated jalapeños
2 large eggs, lightly beaten
1 pound uncooked lasagna noodles
1 cup shredded Parmesan cheese

1. Place the tomatoes in a large saucepan and cover with water. Bring to a boil until the skins crack. Remove the tomatoes with a slotted spoon and place in a colander under cold running water until cool enough to handle. Peel and discard the skins. Place the tomatoes, chopped parsley, basil, spinach, garlic cloves, one of the onions, the diced tomatoes and green chiles, Italian seasoning, salt, black pepper, 2 tablespoons olive oil, and the Worcestershire sauce in a blender. Blend until smooth.

2. In a large skillet over medium heat, cook the ground beef and Italian sausage, stirring occasionally, until the meat begins to brown, about 4 minutes. Stir in the mushrooms, fennel seeds, and red pepper flakes. Cook until the meat has browned, another minute or so.

3. Pour the beef and onion mixture into a large pot and add half of the contents of the blender.

4. In the same skillet used for the meat, melt the butter. Add the remaining onion and cook for 3 minutes over medium heat, or until the onion is tender.

5. Add the tomato paste and reduce the heat to medium-low, stirring constantly, for 2 to 3 minutes. Scrape the tomato paste mixture into the blender. Add 1 tablespoon olive oil and blend until smooth. Pour the contents of the blender into the pot with the beef mixture.

6. Stir in the wine and cook over low heat, stirring occasionally, for 3 hours.

7. Meanwhile, in a medium bowl, mix together the ricotta, diced mozzarella, 2 cups of the shredded mozzarella, the minced parsley, and jalapeños. Stir in the eggs until smooth.

8. Place the lasagna noodles in a large pot and cover with water. Add a pinch of salt and the remaining 1 tablespoon olive oil. Cook for about 4 minutes, or until al dente. Drain the noodles in a colander, then transfer to a large pot of cold water to prevent sticking.

9. Preheat the oven to 375°F.

10. Ladle a thin layer of the meat sauce on the bottom of a large, deep casserole dish or 12-inch Dutch oven. Top with a layer of noodles, about a third of the meat sauce, and a third of the cheese mixture. Arrange another layer of noodles in the opposite direction you placed the first layer, followed by more meat sauce and another covering of the cheese mixture. Repeat until all the ingredients are used.

11. Sprinkle the top with the remaining 2 cups shredded mozzarella, the Parmesan cheese, and, if using, the red pepper flakes.

12. Cover the casserole dish with foil and bake for 25 to 30 minutes. Remove the foil and continue baking for another 25 to 30 minutes, until the top is a light golden brown. Remove from the oven and let rest for 20 minutes before serving.

CALL OF THE COCINERO
MEXICAN-INSPIRED CLASSICS

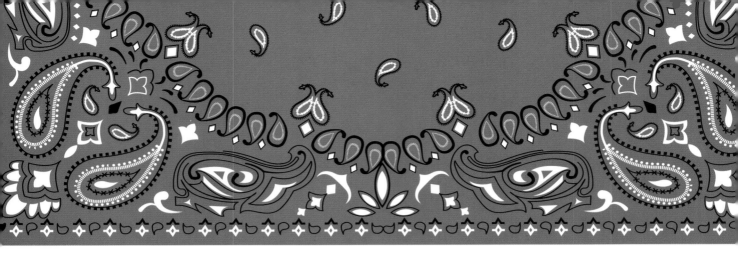

Following the Civil War, thousands of longhorns roamed free in South Texas, Louisiana, Oklahoma, and the New Mexico areas. With the expansion west, the demand to feed folks with beef grew. Thus, the great cattle drives were born.

Herds of fifteen hundred to twenty-five hundred head were gathered by cowboys and driven north to newly established railroad hubs. From there, the beef could be shipped all across the country. Typically, these cowboys ranged in age from late teens to early thirties, but some old-timers would ride the trail too. These cowboys needed to eat during the long trek up to the railheads, so a cook was also part of the crew. His kitchen was fashioned from an old wagon that had a fold-down table and storage for his supplies and equipment. In camp, the cook was the man in charge, and while he was often known to be a cantankerous ol' coot, no one wanted to make the cook mad and risk the chance of him soaping their plate.

Since most drives started in South Texas, a lot of the hired cooks were of Mexican descent, bringing with them their rich culture of food flavored with dried chiles and spices. His dress wasn't the same, nor the crease of his hat, but he had respect on the wagon. He was called the cocinero, or "coosie." I had an old cowboy tell me that his dad told him, "If you ever see a chuck wagon in the distance with a large sombrero flopping in the breeze, you better put your horse in a fast pace and hire on for that outfit, because it's going to be some good eating."

The staples on a chuck wagon would include coffee, flour, sugar, lard, beans, and salt pork. With a Mexican cook, it would also be common to see a burlap bag of dried chiles hanging from the side of the wagon. If he had time, he would rehydrate these chiles for sauces or grind them up for seasoning beans and other otherwise bland dishes. If you had such a cook, chances are you would be traveling with a lot more heat and flavor.

Growing up in the Texas/Oklahoma area, I was also raised with a hearty dose of Mexican-influenced recipes. In fact, cowboys have come to expect not only that our meals are going to be authentic but that some might even bite back! I do love some kick in my food, and the chile de árbol is one of those little peppers that will sneak up on you!

I can remember being in a hurry making some carne guisada, a rich beef stew simmered in poblano and serrano chiles, for lunch one day on a ranch in northern New Mexico. I had ground up some chiles de árbol for the stew. However, I had too many irons in the fire: making corn tortillas, stirring meat, and prepping a dessert. I knew I'd started out with four chiles, but with the wind blowing about thirty-five mph, I also knew that some of the flakes made it into the pot, some were left on the chuck box lid, and the rest probably were in southern Colorado by now. So, with the stew simmering, I went about my chores.

It soon came time to start the caramel apple pie. Brown sugar, flour, and cinnamon got mixed together and tossed in with some fresh apples. I hadn't noticed it before, but as I looked, the apples had a little brown tint to them. I just figured it was a bit of that New Mexico real estate that had blown up, so I placed the lid on the Dutch oven to start cooking the pie.

The cowboys showed up hungry and got them some heaping bowls of the carne guisada. Some ate it as a soup, some spooned it onto their tortillas. It didn't take long before the pot was empty. I set out the Dutch oven full of pie and sliced it up. I always enjoy watching folks take a bite of my desserts because you can usually see that wave of contentment roll across their face with every sweet bite. However, this time was a little different. I noticed some of the boys perk up with a peculiar look on their face, and then sort of glance at each other in confusion. For a while no one said anything, because you never question the cook. But finally, one of the boys worked up the nerve to ask, "Cookie, you reckon these apples grew up next to a jalapeño plant, 'cause they sure got a bite to 'em!" I knew right then where the other remnants of those chiles went. I just looked at him and answered, "Yep, and they might even have been fertilized with gunpowder, so y'all be careful out there horseback."

While the days of the cattle drives are long gone, some of the old wagon tracks can still be seen like deep scars in the red earth. We still follow in these tracks rich in history through recipes and stories, paying homage to all those great cooks who came before us. And when I serve up each dish, I imagine ol' Coosie would have had about the same call as I do now: "Ven a buscarlo antes de que lo tire!" *Come and get it before I throw it out!*

This dish is a bit like nachos that have been cooked in a traditional deep red sauce of dried chiles. Add in a chile de árbol (or more) if you like extra heat! This is typically made using dried corn tortillas, but you could use flour, if you like. Be sure to leave the tortillas out on the counter overnight so they dry out well, which will help them crisp up better when frying. This is topped with a fried egg to make it a unique breakfast dish, but you can serve it up anytime you have a hankering for some traditional Mexican food.

CHILAQUILES

MAKES 4 SERVINGS

PREP TIME: 20 MINUTES

TOTAL TIME: 40 MINUTES

3 dried chiles cascavel, stemmed and seeded

3 dried ancho chiles, stemmed and seeded

3 dried guajillo chiles, stemmed and seeded

3 garlic cloves

4 Roma tomatoes, cored

1 white onion, sliced

1 to 2 chiles de árbol, stemmed and seeded (optional)

3 tablespoons corn oil

8 (8- to 10-inch) corn tortillas

½ tablespoon butter

4 large eggs

Crumbled queso fresco, for topping

Sliced avocado, for topping

1. Place a large cast-iron skillet over high heat. Heat to smoking, then turn off the heat. Add the cascavel, ancho, and guajillo chiles and garlic. Press the peppers down to toast slightly, turning them occasionally, 4 minutes.

2. Place the tomatoes, onion, contents of the skillet, and, if using, the chile(s) de árbol in a large pot and cover with water. Bring to a boil, then turn off the heat and let rest for 15 minutes, or until the chiles soften.

3. Strain the ingredients from the pot and place in a blender. Reserve 1 cup of the liquid and set aside. Blend until smooth.

4. In a large cast-iron skillet, heat the corn oil over medium-high heat.

5. Cut the tortillas into chip-size pieces. Add the chips to the skillet and toss to lightly coat with the oil. Continue cooking until the chips have evenly toasted, stirring frequently, about 8 minutes. Transfer the chips to paper towels to drain.

6. Place the skillet over medium heat and pour in the red sauce. Stir in ¼ to ½ cup of the reserved liquid and cook, stirring constantly, until it comes to a hard simmer, about 5 minutes. Remove from the heat.

7. Toss the tortilla chips into the skillet with the sauce until evenly coated. If the sauce is too thick, add a little more of the reserved liquid, but you don't want the sauce to be too soupy. Cook over medium heat for about 3 minutes, but be careful

Recipe continues ➤

not to overcook or the chips will get soggy. Set aside and keep warm.

8. Melt the butter in a medium skillet over medium heat. Crack in the eggs and cook until they are over easy to over medium, 3 to 6 minutes.

9. Top the chips with the fried eggs, some queso fresco, and sliced avocados. Serve immediately.

> **TIP** Allowing the tortillas to set out for a few hours before cutting will cause them to dry out and fry up faster.

"If you find yourself in a hole, the first thing to do is to stop digging."

Tradition and comfort combine here to give you a taste of tender pork shoulder, hominy, and chiles. This all simmers together in a rich red chile sauce for a south-of-the-border soup. The hominy adds a unique corn flavor that blends well with the peppers and chiles. Perfect for cooler temperatures, this will warm your heart, soul, and stomach.

PORK POZOLE

MAKES ABOUT 10 SERVINGS

PREP TIME: 1 HOUR AND 10 MINUTES
TOTAL TIME: 2 HOURS AND 40 MINUTES

1 (4- to 5-pound) pork shoulder, trimmed and cut into bite-size pieces

1 jalapeño, roasted, peeled, seeded, and sliced

1 serrano chile, roasted, peeled, seeded, and sliced

2 tomatillos, peeled and cored

4 dried ancho chiles, stemmed and seeded

10 dried guajillo chiles, stemmed and seeded

1 dried chile de árbol, stemmed and seeded

1 large white onion, quartered

6 garlic cloves, halved

2 teaspoons dried oregano

1 teaspoon ground cumin

½ tablespoon chili powder

2 chicken bouillon cubes

2 bay leaves

4 (15-ounce) cans white hominy, drained

Coarsely ground salt and black pepper

Shredded cabbage, sliced radish, and/or tortillas, for serving (optional)

1. Pour 12 cups water into a large stew pot and add the pork, jalapeño, and serrano. Cover and cook over medium-high heat for 1 hour. As the mixture cooks, skim off any foam and discard. The more fat the pork has on it, the more foam may appear. Skim it off a few times during the cooking process as needed.

2. Preheat the oven to 400°F.

3. Place the tomatillos on a small baking sheet and bake for 20 minutes, or until they are blistered and tender. Set aside to cool.

4. Place the ancho chiles, guajillo chiles, chile de árbol, and onion in a medium saucepan and cover with water. Bring to a boil over medium-high heat and cook until tender, about 20 minutes.

5. Strain the chiles and onion from the saucepan (discard the liquid) and place in a blender. Add the tomatillos, garlic, oregano, cumin, and chili powder.

6. In a small saucepan over high heat, dissolve the chicken bouillon in 4 cups water. Bring to a boil for a few minutes, then pour ½ cup of the broth into the blender and blend until smooth. Reserve the remaining broth.

7. Strain the contents of the blender into a medium bowl. Stir the strained sauce into the pot with the pork. Stir in the remaining 3½ cups of chicken stock and the bay leaves.

8. Cover and simmer for 45 minutes to 1 hour over medium heat, until the pork is tender. Stir in the hominy and season with salt and pepper to taste. Cover and let simmer for 30 minutes.

9. Discard the bay leaves. Serve topped with shredded cabbage, thinly sliced radishes, and/or tortillas, if desired.

TIP If you prefer a thicker broth, when done cooking, add some corn masa, a little at a time, until you reach the desired thickness.

Now you can enjoy Mexican street food right in your backyard. The name translates to "shepherd-style," inspired by Lebanese immigrants and their lamb shawarma. It has a unique cooking method and is smoked on a vertical spit. We're using tender pork shoulder marinated in an authentic chile sauce that has a little tangy sweetness to it thanks to orange and pineapple juices.

TACOS AL PASTOR

MAKES ABOUT 12 TACOS

PREP TIME: 12 HOURS AND 15 MINUTES

TOTAL TIME: 14 HOURS AND 45 MINUTES

6 dried guajillo chiles

6 dried cascavel chiles

4 garlic cloves

2 white onions, quartered

1 (6- to 7-pound) pork butt, or 4 pounds pork steak

⅓ cup apple cider vinegar

1 cup pineapple juice

1 cup orange juice

Juice of 2 limes

1 cinnamon stick, grated

1 tablespoon dried oregano

½ tablespoon ground cumin

2 tablespoons honey

⅓ cup adobo sauce

1 pineapple, cut into ½-inch-thick rings

1 red onion, sliced into rings

12 corn tortillas

Crumbled queso fresco, for topping

Chopped fresh cilantro, for topping

1. Place the guajillo chiles, cascavel chiles, garlic cloves, and white onions in a large pot. Cover with water and bring to a boil for 10 minutes, or until the peppers are tender.

2. Meanwhile, remove the bone from the pork butt and separate the muscles. (You can also have the butcher do this for you, or use pork steaks instead.) Slice the meat into about ½-inch-thick strips. Set aside.

3. Strain the chiles, garlic, and white onions from the pot and place in a blender. Blend until smooth, then pour the contents into a colander over a large bowl to strain out the stems and seeds. Return the strained sauce to the blender.

4. Add the vinegar, pineapple juice, orange juice, lime juice, cinnamon, oregano, cumin, honey, and adobo sauce to the blender. Blend until well incorporated.

5. Let the mixture cool to room temperature, then pour into a large bowl. Add the meat and toss to coat well. Cover and place in the fridge for at least 12 hours.

6. Clean, oil, and preheat the grill to 350°F. (See "Grate Care" on page 182.) Put 1 pineapple slice on the bottom of a meat stand or vertical spit. Begin stacking the meat by pushing the slices of pork through the skewer. Top with a pineapple ring. Note: You may have leftover meat.

7. Place the meat stand on the indirect heat side of the grill, close the lid, and cook for 1 hour.

8. Rotate the stand 180 degrees and spoon the juices from the bottom of the stand to generously baste the meat. Cook for an additional 1 to 1½ hours, basting every 15 to 20 minutes, until the meat has cooked through.

Recipe continues ➤

9. Move the meat stand over to the far edge of the indirect heat. Add the remaining pineapple slices and the red onion slices to the direct heat side of the grill. Cook on both sides until the onion is tender and the pineapple has good grill marks and char. If you have leftover meat slices, place on the direct heat and cook 3 to 4 minutes per side, or until slightly charred.

10. Remove the onion and pineapple from the grill and roughly chop. Remove the meat stand from the grill and place on a baking sheet. Slice down the stand to cut the meat off about ½ inch thick.

11. Place the tortillas on the grill just until warmed through. Spoon a generous helping of meat, pineapple, and onion on each tortilla and top with some queso fresco cheese and cilantro. Serve warm.

This is not like the Taco Bell version. We're making this more traditional. *Gordita* means "chubby" in Spanish. The dough, made from potato and corn masa, is cut in the middle and filled with a variety of ingredients to be enjoyed as either a sweet or savory dish. We're adding a little bacon, jalapeño, and onion into the dough, then lightly toasting in a cast-iron skillet. Feel free to get creative with the stuffing of this dish. Use seasoned ground beef or beans for a savory filling or fruit preserves and powdered sugar to make it sweet.

GORDITAS

MAKES 6 TO 8 GORDITAS

PREP TIME: 1 HOUR AND 10 MINUTES

TOTAL TIME: 1 HOUR AND 40 MINUTES

¾ cup chicken broth

2 to 2¼ cups instant corn masa flour

2 teaspoons salt

1 teaspoon baking powder

2 medium russet potatoes, peeled

6 slices bacon, chopped

1 white onion, chopped

3 jalapeños, stemmed, seeded, and chopped

2 garlic cloves, minced

1 teaspoon ground cumin

Salt and black pepper

2 tablespoons butter, melted

8 tablespoons crumbled queso fresco, plus more for serving

Table crema and salsa, for topping

1. In a medium saucepan over medium heat, warm the broth with ¾ cup water.

2. In a large bowl, combine 2 cups of the masa, the salt, and baking powder. Slowly begin stirring in the broth until a soft dough that isn't sticky forms. If needed, you can add more masa to achieve the desired consistency. Lightly knead the dough for 2 to 3 minutes with your hands.

3. Leave the dough in the bowl and form a small well in the middle of the dough. Tightly cover the dough with plastic wrap and set aside in a warm place for 45 minutes.

4. Place the potatoes in a large saucepan and cover with water. Bring to a boil over high heat for 10 minutes, or until fork tender. Remove and let

cool slightly. In a medium bowl, roughly mash the potatoes with a fork until slightly chunky.

5. In a large skillet over medium-high heat, cook the bacon until browned, about 5 minutes. Transfer to paper towels to drain. Reserve the grease in the skillet.

6. Add the onion to the skillet and cook, stirring occasionally, until it starts to become tender, about 4 minutes. Stir in the jalapeños and cook, stirring occasionally, until tender, another 4 minutes.

7. Reduce the heat to low and stir in the garlic cloves. Cook until fragrant, about 1 minute. Stir in the mashed potatoes, chopped bacon, and cumin. Season with salt and pepper to taste.

Recipe continues ➤

Cook, stirring occasionally, for about 2 minutes. Remove from the heat.

8. Remove the plastic wrap from the dough and pour the melted butter into the well. Fold the dough and knead until the butter is well incorporated.

9. Pinch off the dough into six to eight 2½-inch balls. Lightly pat the balls to form a small bowl. Spoon a heaping tablespoon of the potato mixture from the skillet onto the dough and add 1 tablespoon of the queso fresco. Fold the dough around the mixture and knead with your hands to incorporate into the dough. Repeat with the remaining dough balls.

10. Place each ball between two sheets of waxed paper and mash down into a 5-inch-wide circle that is about ½ inch thick. Repeat with the remaining balls.

11. Working in batches, in a large cast-iron skillet over low heat, cook the dough disks, flipping occasionally, until they are firm to the touch and lightly browned, 5 to 7 minutes on each side. Remove and set on a wire rack. Continue with the remaining dough.

12. Slice the gorditas halfway down and stuff with the leftover mashed potato filling. Top with queso fresco and, if desired, crema and salsa. Serve immediately.

There are a few things that I judge a good Mexican restaurant by, and they are how full is the parking lot and do they make good cheese enchiladas? Sesame seeds toasted in a skillet is an authentic ingredient along with dried oregano leaves and cumin seeds. Of course, the star of this recipe is the cheese, and we're mixing up Monterey Jack, queso fresco, and some smooth and cool table crema for topping.

CHEESE ENCHILADAS

MAKES 4 SERVINGS

PREP TIME: 45 MINUTES

TOTAL TIME: 55 MINUTES

12 guajillo dried chiles, stemmed and seeded

2 ancho dried chiles, stemmed and seeded

4 dried green or Anaheim chiles, stemmed and seeded

2 dried chiles de árbol, stemmed and seeded

4 garlic cloves

1 tablespoon sesame seeds

2 teaspoons cumin seeds

2 teaspoons dried oregano leaves

4 tablespoons butter

1 large white onion, chopped

2 cups chicken broth (see Tip)

½ tablespoon coarsely ground black pepper

1 cinnamon stick, grated

½ teaspoon allspice

4 to 8 tablespoons avocado oil or olive oil

8 corn tortillas

6 ounces Monterey Jack cheese, sliced

½ cup crumbled queso fresco, plus more for topping

Mexican table crema, for topping

1. Preheat the oven to 350°F.

2. Place the guajillo chiles, ancho chiles, green chiles, and chiles de árbol in a large stockpot. Cover with water and bring to a low boil for 10 minutes, or until tender.

3. Strain the chiles from the pot and place in a blender. Add 1 cup of the chile liquid (discard the rest) and the garlic cloves and blend well. Strain the mixture into a large bowl and set aside.

4. Add the sesame seeds to a medium cast-iron skillet over medium-low heat. Stir frequently until they are lightly toasted. Stir in the cumin and oregano and continue to cook for 1 to 2 minutes, stirring frequently. Remove the seeds and oregano from the skillet and crush with a mortar and pestle.

5. In the same skillet over medium heat, melt 2 tablespoons of the butter. Add the onion and cook, stirring occasionally, until tender, about 4 minutes.

6. In a large cast-iron skillet over medium heat, melt the remaining 2 tablespoons butter. Add the strained red sauce. Stir in the broth, crushed seeds and oregano, pepper, cinnamon, and allspice. Cook for 15 to 20 minutes, until the sauce thickens.

7. In a separate medium skillet over medium heat, warm ½ to 1 tablespoon of the oil. Add the tortillas, a few at a time, and cook 30 seconds per side, or until soft and flexible. Place on a wire rack and repeat with the remaining tortillas.

8. Dip a tortilla in the red sauce, making sure to coat both sides. Lay the tortilla flat on a cutting board. Spoon some onion in the center and add 2 slices of Monterey Jack cheese and 2 tablespoons queso fresco. Tightly roll up and place in the large skillet, seam side down. Repeat with the remaining tortillas.

9. Bake for 10 minutes, or until the cheese has melted and the enchiladas are warmed through.

10. Place on a serving dish and spoon over the leftover red sauce, sprinkle with crumbled queso fresco, and drizzle with the crema. Serve warm.

> **TIP** For a more authentic flavor, use caldo de pollo (a Mexican type of chicken bouillon) dissolved into a broth in place of the regular chicken broth.

A CAMP COOK'S GUIDE TO WEATHER

It was spring 2019. I was on a ranch in Seymour, Texas, located in the area known as Tornado Alley. I've seen my share of tornados and have been closer to them than I wanted at times. None of the camps I've been in have had Wi-Fi, so there were no weather alerts coming to us.

The first evening we came in to set up camp, we got a call from Robb, the ranch owner, who told us, "Kent, you need to get out of camp and come to the house. There is a bad storm coming, and all the big storm chasers are driving by the house. The Weather Channel is calling for an EF4 tornado tracking right in the direction of camp."

As a crow flies, camp was about thirteen miles from his house. I took a good assessment around, and I told him all the birds were still flying around camp and some had even gone to roost near us. I figured the birds knew more than the news, so we'd be fine staying where we were. I also don't like leaving the wagon, and I was pretty sure the way the clouds were tracking that it was going to go north of us.

We did take down the wagon's fly and secured the ropes on the teepee well before going to bed. The wind did blow, and the hail did fly in sideways, but our teepee was still standing the next morning.

At breakfast, Robb told me that I was crazy for making Shannon stay in camp in the storms. I told him, "We didn't have any damage, how about you?" He laughed, and though he hated to admit it, he said, "I lost most of the shingles on one side of the roof and the hail broke some windows." I told him, "I bet you there weren't any birds hanging around there 'cause they sure don't watch TV!"

The good Lord knows that we don't get the Weather Channel out in the middle of nowhere when we're cooking. I've learned sometimes it's best to rely on Mother Nature to help with weather predictions. So the next time you find yourself in the wild with no connection to the outside world, just look to nature; she's been doing this longer than any news station.

Do you have a hankering for tamales but don't feel like doing all the work? Well, I have you fixed up! My mother and I made this dish together, and I've made it a lot on ranches because it's easy to fix for a crew and you still get all that great traditional corn flavor without all the work. We're using ground beef, green chiles, and hominy, all topped with a corn masa crust.

TAMALE PIE

MAKES ABOUT 6 SERVINGS

PREP TIME: 15 MINUTES

TOTAL TIME: 45 MINUTES

2 pounds ground beef

1 large white onion, chopped

1 red bell pepper, chopped

1 jalapeño, diced

4 garlic cloves, minced

Salt and black pepper

1 (15.5-ounce) can yellow hominy, drained

1 (15-ounce) can crushed tomatoes

2 (4-ounce) cans chopped green chiles

1 tablespoon cornstarch

2 teaspoons chili powder

1 teaspoon ground cumin

1 teaspoon dried oregano

2 cups shredded cheddar cheese

2¼ cups instant corn masa flour

2 teaspoons baking powder

1 teaspoon salt

2 cups chicken broth, plus more if needed

1 stick butter, melted

1. Preheat the oven to 350°F.

2. In a large cast-iron skillet over medium heat, cook the beef, stirring occasionally, until it begins to brown, about 4 minutes. Stir in the onion, bell pepper, jalapeño, and garlic. Continue cooking until the meat has completely browned and the onion is tender, another minute or so. Drain the grease and discard. Return the beef and vegetable mixture to the skillet and season with salt and pepper to taste.

3. Stir in the hominy, tomatoes, green chiles, cornstarch, chili powder, cumin, and oregano. Stir in 1½ cups of the shredded cheese until just combined. Set aside and keep warm.

4. In a large bowl, combine the corn masa, baking powder, and salt. Stir in the broth and melted butter. You want the mixture to hold together but spread easily. Add more broth, if needed.

5. Evenly spread the masa mixture on top of the skillet. Bake for 30 minutes, or until a toothpick inserted into the center of the corn batter comes out clean. Top with the remaining ½ cup of cheese and continue baking until the cheese has melted. Serve warm.

I was introduced to the best rice in Silver City, New Mexico, while I was guiding elk hunters. Before we headed back to the mountains after restocking supplies, my uncle took me down a long alley to a hole-in-the-wall Mexican restaurant. I was served the best rice and beans I had ever eaten, and the old Mexican cook there told me his tips for good rice. You have to rinse the rice well until the water runs clear and then toast it before you start cooking. Don't rush the cooking process—it is worth the wait.

ARROZ ROJO

MAKES 4 SERVINGS

PREP TIME: 10 MINUTES

TOTAL TIME: 40 MINUTES

2 garlic cloves

1 to 2 serrano chiles, stemmed and seeded

1 Roma tomato, cored and halved

½ small white onion, chopped

½ teaspoon dried oregano

½ teaspoon ground cumin

1 dried ancho chile, crushed

3 tablespoons corn oil

1 cup uncooked long-grain white rice, rinsed well

2½ teaspoons chicken bouillon powder

Salt and black pepper

1. Roast the garlic, serrano, and tomato halves over a flame or in a cast-iron skillet, rotating until evenly blistered and slightly charred. Transfer to a blender.

2. Add the onion, oregano, cumin, ancho chile, and ¼ cup warm water to the blender and blend until smooth.

3. In a large saucepan or cast-iron skillet with a tight lid, heat the corn oil over medium-high heat. Stir in the rice and lightly toast, stirring occasionally, about 4 minutes.

4. Stir in the pepper sauce, 1½ cups warm water, and the chicken bouillon. Bring to a boil, stirring constantly. Cover and reduce the heat to low. Cook for 20 minutes. Do not lift the lid.

5. Turn off the heat and remove the lid to release the steam. Quickly replace the lid and let rest for 10 minutes. Fluff the rice with a fork and season with salt and pepper to taste. Serve warm.

This is a traditional stew of sorts but can be served up in a variety of ways. Chuck roast is cut thinly, browned, and simmered until fork tender. Smoked poblanos, serranos, and tomatoes all marinate together to give this stew a hint of heat. You can serve this alone as a stew or over mashed potatoes or rice. I also like to strain it from the broth and spoon onto tortillas.

CARNE GUISADA

MAKES ABOUT 6 SERVINGS

PREP TIME: 40 MINUTES

TOTAL TIME: 1 HOUR AND 40 MINUTES

2½ pounds chuck roast, cut into 1 x 2-inch thin strips

Salt and black pepper

1 tablespoon butter

1 tablespoon avocado oil or olive oil

2 white onions, chopped

2 serrano chiles, diced

4 garlic cloves, minced

2 tablespoons all-purpose flour

3 teaspoons ground cumin

3 teaspoons dried oregano leaves

3 Roma tomatoes, roasted and roughly chopped

2 Anaheim or green chiles, roasted, peeled, seeded, and cut into thin strips

3 poblano chiles, roasted, peeled, seeded, and cut into thin strips

1. Place the meat in a large bowl. Season well with salt and black pepper.

2. In a 12-inch Dutch oven or large pot over medium heat, melt the butter with the oil. Add the meat to the oven or pot. Reduce the heat to medium-low and cover. Cook, stirring occasionally, for about 20 minutes.

3. Spoon out the broth from the meat and reserve. Continue to cook the meat, uncovered, stirring occasionally, until it browns, about 5 minutes.

4. Add the onions, serranos, and garlic. Cook, stirring occasionally, until the onions are tender, about 5 minutes.

5. Reduce the heat to low and evenly sift in the flour. Stir to coat the meat and cook for an additional 4 minutes.

6. Stir in the reserved broth, ½ cup water, cumin, oregano, and tomatoes. Stir in the Anaheim and poblano chiles.

7. Increase the heat to medium, cover, and cook, stirring occasionally, for 45 minutes to 1 hour. You may need to add more water to give this additional moisture as it cooks. You want the meat to be fork tender. Serve warm as a soup, with refried beans, in a tortilla, or over rice or mashed potatoes.

This is the king of truck stop fare to me. I have become quite the convenience store connoisseur, and I know who serves the freshest chimis and burritos on all the stops on the interstate. Chicken, cheese, and green chiles all come together when seasoned with smoked paprika, chili powder, and cumin. If you can find them, use Hatch green chiles, as they will have the best flavor. Wrap 'em up, fry 'em up, and let's have the best handheld meal you've ever wrapped a lip around.

GREEN CHILE AND CHICKEN CHIMICHANGAS

MAKES 6 SERVINGS

PREP TIME: 20 MINUTES

TOTAL TIME: 30 MINUTES

2 large boneless, skinless chicken breasts

Salt and black pepper

1 chicken bouillon cube

½ tablespoon smoked paprika

2 teaspoons ancho chile powder

2 teaspoons ground cumin

2 teaspoons dried oregano

2 (4-ounce) cans diced green chiles

12 thick-cut slices Monterey Jack cheese

6 (10-inch) flour tortillas

12 thick-cut slices Colby Jack cheese

Oil, for frying

1. Place the chicken in a medium pot and cover with water. Stir in the salt and pepper and the bouillon cube. Bring to a boil. Cover and cook about 10 minutes, or until the chicken is cooked through and fork tender. Remove the chicken and set aside to cool. Reserve about ⅓ cup of the broth.

2. When cool enough to handle, shred the chicken with forks or cut into bite-size pieces. Place the shredded chicken in a medium saucepan. Stir in the paprika, ancho chile powder, cumin, oregano, green chiles, and ⅓ cup reserved broth. Cook over medium-low heat, stirring occasionally, to incorporate the flavors, about 4 minutes.

3. Place 2 slices of the Monterey Jack down the middle of a tortilla. Evenly spoon the chicken mixture down the middle. Top with 2 slices of the Colby Jack cheese.

4. Fold the short ends in and then fold the long ends to meet around the middle. Be sure the ends are sealed well. Repeat with the remaining ingredients.

5. In a large cast-iron skillet, heat about ½ inch of oil to 350°F.

6. Place the chimichangas, seam side down, in the skillet. Cook about 3 minutes per side, or until golden brown. Remove and let cool slightly on a wire rack. Serve warm.

Ground beef seasoned with oregano and cumin is a great base for this recipe. The trick to cooking the peppers to perfection is adding a little chicken broth to a pan while cooking. The steam helps the peppers soften better. We're layering the inside of each pepper with cheese, meat, green chiles, and more cheese!

CHEESY CHILE-STUFFED PEPPERS

MAKES 4 SERVINGS

PREP TIME: 20 MINUTES

TOTAL TIME: 45 MINUTES

4 assorted bell peppers

¼ cup chicken broth

1 pound ground beef

½ yellow onion, diced

½ teaspoon dried oregano

½ teaspoon ground cumin

Salt and black pepper

¾ cup shredded cheddar cheese

4 Anaheim or green chiles, roasted, peeled, and diced

¾ cup shredded mozzarella cheese

1. Preheat the oven to 350°F.

2. Cut the tops off the bell peppers and core. Place the peppers in a medium baking pan and pour the broth in the pan. Bake for 15 minutes, or until the peppers begin to soften.

3. In a medium skillet over medium-high heat, cook the beef, stirring occasionally, until it begins to brown, about 4 minutes. Stir in the onion, oregano, and cumin and continue cooking until the meat has completely browned, another minute or so. Drain the grease and discard. Return the beef and onion mixture to the skillet and season with salt and pepper to taste.

4. Remove the peppers from the oven. Increase the heat to 375°F. Reserve at least 3 tablespoons of the liquid in the baking pan. Drain and discard the rest.

5. Evenly stuff each pepper with about 2 tablespoons of cheddar cheese followed by a fourth of the diced Anaheim chiles, about ½ cup meat, and 2 tablespoons mozzarella cheese.

6. Return the peppers to the baking pan and bake for 20 minutes, or until the peppers have completely softened. Remove from the oven and top each pepper with 1 tablespoon of mozzarella cheese and 1 tablespoon of cheddar cheese. Bake for an additional 2 to 3 minutes to melt the cheese. Serve warm.

These will complete any dish that might ask for a corn tortilla. I know it's tempting to just go buy them at the store, but these tortillas really are easy with only four ingredients. I like to fry them up in a little bacon grease instead of oil for more flavor . . . and who doesn't like a little bacon?

EASY CORN TORTILLAS

MAKES ABOUT 10 TORTILLAS

PREP TIME: 15 MINUTES
TOTAL TIME: 30 MINUTES

2 cups instant corn masa flour, plus more as needed

2 teaspoons salt

2½ tablespoons corn oil or bacon grease

1. In a medium bowl, combine the masa and salt. Stir in 1½ cups water. Mix well until a soft ball forms. You may need to add more water or masa to achieve the consistency. The dough should be pliable and soft but not sticky.

2. Form a well in the middle of the dough and add the corn oil. Knead the oil into the dough for about 4 minutes. Cover and let rest for 2 minutes.

3. Pinch off the dough in large golf ball–size balls. Use a tortilla press or rolling pin to roll out the balls to 4½- to 5-inch rounds.

4. In a large cast-iron skillet over medium-high heat, heat ½ tablespoon of oil. Fry 2 tortillas at a time, until light golden brown, 1 to 2 minutes per side. Be sure to not overcook or they will become brittle and fall apart.

TIP These can be stored in a plastic bag in the fridge for up to 10 days. Reheat in a hot skillet with a little oil.

"Don't let your yearnings get ahead of your earnings."

You're probably thinking, *Let's get the Crock-Pot out and cook this pork shoulder until it's tender.* Well, you can, but, folks, there is so much more flavor when it is cooked on the smoker. I love to use oak- and cherrywood with pork. (See Top Tips for Grilling on page 181.) After initial smoking, baste in a mix of lime and orange juice for a tangy flavor that will help tenderize the meat. The best part is crisping up the pork in a cast-iron skillet after smoking for a slight crunch—it's great in a taco.

CARNITAS WITH SMOKED PULLED PORK

MAKES ABOUT 8 TO 10 SERVINGS

PREP TIME: 6 HOURS AND 30 MINUTES

TOTAL TIME: 12 HOURS AND 50 MINUTES

2 tablespoons ground cumin

1 tablespoon dried oregano

1 tablespoon coarsely ground pepper

1 tablespoon sea salt

2 tablespoons dry mustard

1 tablespoon onion powder

1 tablespoon garlic powder

1 tablespoon smoked paprika

2 tablespoons crushed dried ancho chile

2 tablespoons orange zest

1 (6- to 7-pound) pork butt or pork shoulder

Juice of 1 lime

Juice of 2 oranges

4 tablespoons avocado oil or olive oil

Tortillas, shredded cheese, sliced avocados, for serving (optional)

1. In a small bowl, mix together the dry herbs and spices and the orange zest.

2. Pat the pork dry with paper towels. Generously rub the seasoning on the pork to coat well. Cover and place in the fridge for at least 6 hours or up to overnight. Remove the pork from the fridge about 30 minutes before cooking.

3. Clean and oil the grill or smoker. Light hardwood lump charcoal and let the smoker or grill heat to 250° to 270°F. When the coals are white, add two large handfuls of hickory chips. Place the pork on the smoker and smoke for about 4 hours, or until the internal temperature of the pork reaches 160°F.

4. Remove the pork from the smoker and place on a double layer of heavy foil. Bend the ends of the foil up to create a boat around the pork.

5. In a small bowl, combine the lime juice and orange juice. Pour over the pork and wrap with the foil to seal completely.

6. Add four or five more pieces of lump charcoal and a handful of hickory chips to the smoker and return the wrapped pork to the smoker. Cook for 1½ to 2 hours, until the internal temperature is about 190°F. Remove the pork from the smoker and let rest until cool enough to handle.

Recipe continues ➤

7. Unwrap the pork and place it with the juice in a large pan with sidewalls. With a set of forks, shred the pork, mixing it in with the juices.

8. In a large cast-iron skillet over medium-high heat, heat 2 tablespoons of the oil. Place about half the shredded pork in the skillet and cook until the pieces have crisped up slightly, 8 to 10 minutes. Repeat with the remaining oil and pork.

9. Serve in tortillas topped with cheese and avocados, if desired.

"The only time I've been seated in first class wasn't on a plane—but in the seat of a wagon."

8 SECONDS TO SUPPERTIME
COWBOY CAFÉ CLASSICS

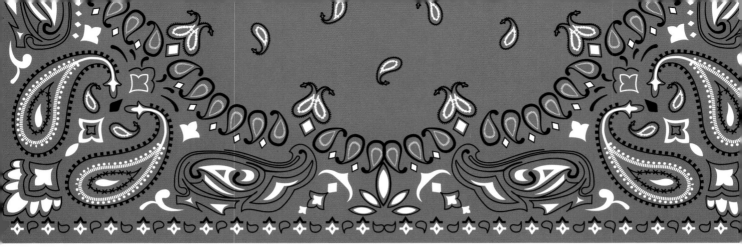

I was on the rodeo circuit a lot back in the early 1980s and was competing every weekend. I rode bulls and won just enough to keep me fueled and fed for another weekend of what I hoped was an eight-second paycheck. Fuel was a lot cheaper then, and as far as being fed well, it sure wasn't fine dining. My youngest son, Jason, who was four years old at the time, went with me nearly every weekend. He soon figured out that the only time we were going to stop was when the gas tank was empty. It was a quick refuel, restroom, and a stale piece of pizza or burrito.

One weekend we were on our way to McLean, Texas, to one of the best open rodeos in the Panhandle. They paid well and gave out buckles to the winner in each event. It had rained all the way on our drive down there, and the radio in that old Ford kept announcing storm warnings for the McLean area to seek shelter. Jason looked at me and said, "Can they still have a rodeo in a tornado?" I laughed and told him as long as there is one light pole left and someplace to park, it will be just right.

When we pulled into town, the rodeo gods were shining down on us. The sun came sparkling through a dark curtain of rain, and there was even a rainbow to the west. When we rounded the corner to the rodeo grounds, it was as if those grounds had turned into a lake. All we needed was a boat and some oars and we could paddle all the way to the other end. But mud doesn't hurt as badly when you hit it going forty mph as dry ground does when you get bucked off.

We climbed to the top of the announcer stand, paid the fees, and found out what I had drawn to ride that night. "H8," the secretary said. "And if you want to know, he ain't been rode this year." Well, that means one of two things: He can sure enough buck, or nobody has given him a gallant effort.

Bull riding is always the last event in a rodeo. "Reckon we could get a burger or hot dog before this starts?" Jason asked. I told him, "Son, we're just eight seconds from suppertime if you can just hold on." He grinned and said, "On the way home, we're going to a sit-down eating place after you win!" I told him he could sure count on it. All I had to do was hang tough for eight seconds.

I was the last rider called when it came time for the bull-riding event. The bad news was those previous fifteen riders had turned the rodeo grounds into a mud bowl for bucking bovines.

With a pull of the rope from a friend and the grin of a four-year-old boy, I figured it was time to meet my dancing partner. Even though he was a rank bull, it felt like riding a rocking chair. It was just one of those moments when you're in the right place at the right time and everything just clicks.

Before I knew it, eight seconds were over and I could hear the blow of the horn. Then came the time to figure out where the exit row was on this flying carpet ride. Right when I felt a good time to eject, he switched directions on me and I face-planted in the deepest mud hole in the arena. I popped up and quickly jumped on the front of the chute. Safe I was. Clean I wasn't. I got most of the dirt and organic matter off my face as everyone was congratulating me and patting me on the back. Most of the good wishes came from kids in their early twenties. They called me the old-timer because I was nearly thirty.

I climbed the stairs to the office to collect my winnings. The secretary handed me the check and looked down at Jason and said, "You reckon you can hold this buckle for your dad?" So with the check in hand and a little feller totin' a new Gist buckle, we made our way to the truck. As we got down the road, Jason said, "My gosh, Daddy, that was a great ride and I'm proud of you! Could we stop at the café down the road and have a real meal?"

"I reckon we earned it," I replied.

We pulled into a little diner and found a spot in an old vinyl booth with duct tape covering some of the holes. I ordered me a big ol' patty melt, and when the waitress brought over our meals, I remember thinking, *This sure beats any two-day-old truck-stop burrito.*

For a moment, we took a break from the road and just enjoyed some good comfort food. It wasn't high dollar, but we both felt like kings eating it. I leaned over to Jason and said, "That eight seconds to suppertime was worth the wait, wasn't it?"

With our bellies full, we loaded in the truck, and not even two miles down the road, my riding partner was out like a light. From that point on, if I won, we'd stopped at an old diner for a sit-down meal and a stand-up time.

FADING TRAILS

You can barely make them out anymore, but along the historic cattle drive trails, such as the Chisolm and Great Western, there are still the remnants of widened river crossings caused by herds of longhorns and deep wagon ruts that cut through the red dirt. With the expansion of railheads, it was more profitable for ranchers to sell their beef in different markets, such as Chicago and New York, which is how the great cattle drives began. During its peak, from 1867 to 1884, more than five million cattle and horses moved along the Chisholm Trail alone. The Great Western Trail came about because the Chisholm Trail had been overused and overgrazed. The Great Western ran parallel to the Chisholm but was a longer trail, starting near Kerrville, Texas, then headed north through nine states. The Great Western Trail began in 1874 and saw its last drive in 1893, and more than seven million head of cattle and horses traveled it north. It was the greatest migration of livestock in world history.

Along these two trails were major stopping points to restock the wagon with supplies. On the Chisholm Trail, one notable stop was the Fleetwood Store, once located on the Red River near Terrel, Oklahoma. The cook would get basic staples, such as flour, coffee, salt pork, and beans, and also wagon parts and the mail.

While these trails had a significant impact in American history, they were short lived because the invention of a thing known as thorny wire was making its way across the once expansive lands of the prairies. With too few trees to build wooden fences, settlers began experimenting with wire. However, a simple wire fence could not keep a thousand-pound longhorn from a green pasture, and that's when various types of "spiked fencing," or barbs, came into play between 1867 and 1874. In 1876, three million pounds of barbed wire were being manufactured, and by 1895, the entire Texas Panhandle had been fenced. Native Americans called it the devil's rope, as it ensnared wild buffalo.

Yet this seemed like the perfect solution for early settlers who didn't want a big herd of cattle grazing and tromping down their crops. Toward the end of the trail days, trail drivers made negotiations with and payments to landowners in order to move cattle across their properties.

By the late 1890s, the stretching of barbed wire and more homesteads were the death of the open range. Today, the great drives no longer exist. Trucking has taken the place of railways, and cattle can even be sold on the internet. But cowboys are still out there taking care of livestock and land. And if they're out there, well, they need a cook.

I was fortunate enough to get to cook for the marking of the Great Western Trail in May 2004, at Doan's Crossing between Altus, Oklahoma, and Vernon, Texas. This also marked the 125th anniversary of the Chisholm Trail. It was like standing on sacred ground, and I could still see the wide crossing on the banks of the Red River. I thought to myself, as the sun was just coming up, just how many old cooks had been in this same spot. I could almost hear them longhorns bellering and the whooping and hollering of

cowboys riding across. I've wished many times that I could have gone down these trails back then to see the land before the fence and the plow. To see this great unsettled country from a wagon seat would be a journey you wouldn't forget.

The Great Trails may be only on old maps now, but they still live on in the hearts of cooks and cowboys and those who blazed a trail to feed beef to America.

Oklahoma is known for more than just the musical and the blowing wind! Oklahomans have enjoyed fried onion burgers since Ross Davis created them in the early 1920s. He was trying to figure a way around the high cost of beef, and onions were cheap. Less meat and more onions still allow for a feller to get full, and it don't sacrifice any of the flavor either. The sweetness of the caramelized onions and our sauce made with French onion dip create the perfect homage to this Oklahoma classic.

OKLAHOMA FRIED ONION BURGER

MAKES 4 HAMBURGERS

PREP TIME: 50 MINUTES

TOTAL TIME: 2 HOURS AND 5 MINUTES

½ cup French onion dip

1 to 2 tablespoons yellow mustard

2 teaspoons Worcestershire sauce

2 large yellow onions, thinly sliced

Coarsely ground salt

1 pound 80% lean ground beef

4 tablespoons butter

Salt and black pepper

4 hamburger buns

4 slices cheddar cheese

Pickles, for serving (optional)

1. In a small bowl, whisk together the onion dip, mustard, and Worcestershire sauce. Adjust the ingredients to taste as desired. Cover and place in the fridge until ready to serve.

2. Place the onions in a colander over a large bowl. Generously sprinkle the onions with salt and toss. Let the onions sit 30 to 45 minutes so the moisture drains.

3. Dump the onions out onto a clean cloth towel and press to absorb any leftover moisture. Set aside.

4. Form the ground beef into 4 equal-size balls.

5. In a large cast-iron skillet over medium heat, melt the butter. Place the beef balls in the skillet and, with a flat spatula or burger press, flatten the meat into thin patties. Let cook 1 to 2 minutes.

6. Place a heaping amount of the onions on top of each patty. Season the tops with salt and pepper.

7. Continue cooking until the patties begin to brown along the outside edge. Carefully flip the patties over so the onions are on the bottom.

8. Cook for about 3 minutes, then place the bottom bun, upside down, on top of the patty. Place the top bun on top of the bottom bun and leave for 2 to 3 minutes to allow both buns to steam as the meat cooks.

9. Remove the buns and place a slice of cheese on top of each patty. Continue cooking until the cheese melts.

10. Place the bottom bun on top of the burger and carefully flip the burger onto the bun and remove from the skillet. Repeat with the remaining burgers. Spread a generous amount of the French onion dip mixture on the top bun and place on top. Serve immediately.

This is a take on a Dairy Queen and Texas fast-food-chain classic, where I've enjoyed many a meal while on the road. The Steak Finger Basket is always my go-to order. Shan always asks, "Aren't you going to change it up?" My answer is no. Why change horses in the middle of the race when you're riding a winner? We're tenderizing good round steaks and dipping them in a lightly seasoned batter that will stick to the meat and your ribs. You can ask your butcher to tenderize the steaks for you, or you can do it yourself with a meat hammer, which will ensure a tender bite.

STEAK FINGERS

MAKES ABOUT 4 SERVINGS

PREP TIME: 15 MINUTES

TOTAL TIME: 30 MINUTES

3 (5-ounce) cubed round steaks

2 cups all-purpose flour

3 tablespoons cornstarch

1 tablespoon baking powder

½ tablespoon garlic powder

½ tablespoon seasoned salt

½ tablespoon black pepper

2 large eggs

1½ cups buttermilk

Oil, for frying

1. Cut the steaks into 1-inch strips and set aside.

2. In a medium bowl, combine the flour, 2 tablespoons of the cornstarch, baking powder, garlic powder, seasoned salt, and pepper.

3. In a separate bowl, whisk together the eggs, buttermilk, and the remaining 1 tablespoon cornstarch.

4. In a large saucepan or Dutch oven, heat about 3 inches of oil to 350°F.

5. Dredge the meat strips in the flour mixture and then dip in the buttermilk mixture, coating generously. Repeat back in the flour mixture, then buttermilk mixture, finishing in the flour mixture. Gently shake off any excess coating and set on a wire rack for at least 3 minutes to let the batter and flour dry. This will help the batter stick to the meat.

6. Fry the strips until golden brown, 3 to 4 minutes. Place them on a wire rack to cool slightly. Serve warm.

I sure think that if you sit down at a diner and a patty melt isn't on the menu, then you aren't at a true all-American diner! The caramelized onions are what make this dish unique, and adding a little vinegar to those onions gives them a good golden-brown color when cooking. Find yourself good pieces of Texas Toast because that will provide heartiness to this sandwich, and it'll toast up to perfection.

TEXAS TOAST PATTY MELT

MAKES 2 PATTY MELTS

PREP TIME: 5 MINUTES
TOTAL TIME: 40 MINUTES

4 tablespoons butter

1 large sweet yellow onion, thinly sliced

2 tablespoons Worcestershire sauce

1 pound 80% lean ground beef

Salt and black pepper

Spicy Mustard Sauce (recipe follows)

2 pieces Texas Toast or thick-cut bread

2 slices Swiss cheese

2 slices pepper jack cheese

Mayonnaise, for spreading

1. In a medium cast-iron skillet over medium-low heat, melt 2 tablespoons of the butter. Add the onion and cook, stirring occasionally, until the onion has caramelized and reached a deep golden brown color, about 20 minutes.

2. Remove the onion from the skillet with a slotted spoon and transfer to a small bowl. Stir in the Worcestershire sauce. Cover and set aside.

3. Divide the ground beef into 2 equal pieces and form each into a rectangular shape that is larger than the bread slices and about $1/8$ to $1/4$ inch thick, to allow for shrinkage while cooking. Season both sides of the patties with salt and pepper.

4. In the same skillet the onion was in, melt the remaining 2 tablespoons of the butter over medium heat. Add the beef patties and cook for 2 to 3 minutes. Mash the burgers down slightly with a spatula. Flip and continue cooking for 2 minutes, or until cooked through. Remove from the skillet.

5. Spread a generous amount of the sauce on a slice of the bread. Top with 1 slice of the Swiss cheese, half of the onions, 1 slice of the pepper jack cheese, and a burger patty. Top with a second bread slice. Repeat to make the second patty melt.

6. Spread a thin layer of mayonnaise on the outside bread slices and place back in the skillet over medium heat. Toast each side for 2 to 3 minutes, mashing down slightly with a spatula. Serve immediately.

SPICY MUSTARD SAUCE

⅓ cup mayonnaise

1 tablespoon spicy mustard

1 tablespoon BBQ sauce

1 tablespoon ketchup

1 jalapeño, grated

In a mixing bowl, whisk together all the ingredients until smooth.

We added an *A* in there, because that sliced avocado was feeling left out. This is a simple recipe, but the fresh ingredients are what make this easy sandwich stand out. Thick-cut bacon that has been rubbed down with coarsely ground black pepper is the star of the show. A juicy beefsteak tomato sprinkled with a little brown sugar gives this sandwich a unique sweetness. Finally, we're spreading it with a little smoky mayo for a Western flavor.

ULTIMATE BLTA

MAKES 2 SANDWICHES

PREP TIME: 30 MINUTES

TOTAL TIME: 45 MINUTES

¾ cup mayonnaise

3 teaspoons chili powder

1 teaspoon smoked paprika

2 teaspoons Worcestershire sauce

8 slices thick-cut bacon

Coarsely ground black pepper

1 large beefsteak tomato, sliced

4 tablespoons packed light brown sugar

Butter, for spreading

4 slices sourdough bread

2 avocados, sliced

Butter lettuce, for topping

1. In a small bowl, whisk together the mayonnaise, chili powder, paprika, and Worcestershire sauce. Cover and place in the fridge for at least 30 minutes before serving.

2. Lay the bacon in a single layer on a baking sheet. Generously coat both sides with pepper. Cover and place in the fridge for 30 minutes.

3. Remove the bacon from the fridge and place in a large cast-iron skillet. Fry over medium-high heat until done but not too crispy, 4 to 5 minutes. Transfer to paper towels to drain. (Alternatively, you can bake the bacon at 400°F for 10 minutes, or until done.)

4. Sprinkle both sides of the tomato slices with brown sugar. Cover and set aside.

5. Spread the butter on both sides of the bread. Place in a cast-iron skillet and toast both sides until golden brown.

6. To assemble the sandwich, spread a layer of the mayonnaise sauce on the bottom slice of the bread, add 4 pieces of bacon, a layer of avocado, butter lettuce, and a couple of tomato slices. Spread more mayonnaise sauce on the top bread slice, if desired, and place on top of the sandwich. Repeat for the second sandwich. Serve immediately.

The first thing I think of when I see this title is *Make sure you have plenty of napkins, don't wear a white shirt, and be cautious!* But, folks, it is so worth it, because in our recipe we are saving you money on napkins and laundry since we've thickened up the chili to stay on the dog. You know me—we're also adding in some southwestern spices to enhance the traditional chili flavor, along with some homemade spicy mustard sauce with jalapeños and sweet relish for a sweet bite.

CHILI CHEESE DOG

MAKES 8 SERVINGS

PREP TIME: 5 MINUTES

TOTAL TIME: 1 HOUR

2 pounds 80% lean ground beef

½ tablespoon ancho chile powder

2 tablespoons chili powder

2 teaspoons ground cumin

2 teaspoons smoked paprika

1 teaspoon dried oregano

2 teaspoons garlic powder

Salt and black pepper

½ cup beef broth

2 cups shredded cheddar cheese

8 hot dogs

8 hot dog buns

Mustard Sauce (recipe follows)

1. In a large pot over medium heat, crumble in the ground beef. Stir in the ancho chile powder, chili powder, cumin, paprika, oregano, and garlic powder. Season with salt and pepper. Drain and discard excess grease, if needed.

2. Cook for about 10 minutes, stirring occasionally. Stir in the broth and reduce the heat to medium-low. Cook for 30 minutes, stirring occasionally.

3. Stir in ½ cup of the cheese. If needed, add more cheese to thicken the mixture so it's not too soupy. Set aside and keep warm.

4. Clean, oil, and preheat the grill to medium-high. (See "Grate Care" on page 182.) Place the hot dogs on the grill and cook for 4 to 5 minutes, rolling them around the grill until lightly charred on all sides. (Alternatively, this can be done in a cast-iron skillet on the stovetop.)

5. Place the buns on the grill, open side up. Sprinkle enough cheese to cover the bottom of each bun, about 2 tablespoons. Top with about 1 to 2 tablespoons of the mustard sauce. Let the buns warm on the grill for 2 to 3 minutes, or until the cheese is melted. Top each bun with a hot dog, chili, and about 1 tablespoon cheese. Serve immediately.

MUSTARD SAUCE

MAKES ABOUT ¾ CUP

PREP TIME: 5 MINUTES

TOTAL TIME: 35 MINUTES

½ cup spicy mustard

2 tablespoons ketchup

1 tablespoon mayonnaise

1 tablespoon diced jalapeño

1½ tablespoons sweet relish

In a small bowl, whisk together the mustard, ketchup, mayonnaise, jalapeño, and sweet relish. Cover and place in the fridge for at least 30 minutes before serving.

This staple can be found at any state fair from Texas to Minnesota. And when I was rodeoing so many years ago, this was my go-to grab at the truck stop. Now granted, they had probably been in the warmer for about two days, but I still craved that buttery corn and dog! The batter is key here, and we're using a little honey to add some sweetness and a little caramelization flavor as it cooks. Some grated jalapeño and onion round out the savory flavor.

HOMEMADE CORN DOGS

MAKES 8 SERVINGS

PREP TIME: 10 MINUTES

TOTAL TIME: 25 MINUTES

8 hot dogs

Wooden corn dog sticks

1½ cups yellow cornmeal

1¼ cups all-purpose flour

1 teaspoon garlic powder

2 tablespoons baking powder

3 tablespoons light brown sugar

1 teaspoon salt

1 teaspoon black pepper

1 large egg

1 tablespoon avocado oil or olive oil

1¾ cups buttermilk

⅓ cup honey

¼ cup grated white onion

¼ cup grated jalapeño

Oil, for frying

1. Pat the hot dogs dry with paper towels. Insert the corn dog sticks at least halfway through one end of each hot dog. Place the hot dogs on a wire rack and set aside.

2. In a medium bowl, combine the cornmeal, flour, garlic powder, baking powder, brown sugar, and salt and pepper.

3. In a separate medium bowl, whisk together the egg, oil, buttermilk, and honey.

4. Pour the wet mixture into the dry mixture and whisk well. Stir in the onion and jalapeño.

5. In a large saucepan or Dutch oven, heat about 3 inches of oil to 350°F. Be sure the cooking vessel is large enough for the hot dog(s) and their sticks to lie flat while frying.

6. Pour the batter into a tall glass. Dip the hot dogs in and swirl the stick around for an even coating.

7. Place the hot dogs sideways in the oil, so the hot dog and stick are lying flat in the oil. Cook until golden brown, rolling around for an even browning, 3 to 4 minutes. Remove and place on a wire rack. Serve warm.

THE SUPER LOOPER

There's a saying in our part of the country: "If you got it tied on your saddle, you better know how to use it." I was fortunate in life to grow up around some of the best cowboys in these parts, and believe me, those fellers could handle a rope.

Ropes sure have changed throughout the years. From the old-school nylon ropes, thirty-three feet in length, to the newfangled poly ropes in every color of the rainbow. Growing up, they were all the old-style grass ropes. With those ropes, if it was too hot in the summer, you could dip them in a stock tank to stiffen them up. When it was too cold, we'd put them close to a branding fire to warm up. I remember my older brother even placing his in the oven to get it just right . . . I don't think Mama knew.

Anyway, let's get back to roping. I admired those old-timers. To see them lay a heel loop just right, or throw a houlihan* when roping horses out, they never seemed to miss. Roping was something I practiced nearly every day when I was young. I roped dogs, chickens, buckets, and anvils. Anything that stood still or gave me a chance, I tried to put a loop around it. However, roping on the ground is different from on horseback. It takes a lot more practice to hit a moving target when you're moving as well.

My older brother, Randy, had been around all those cowboys we called *super loopers*, men who could rope anything from any angle while sitting or standing on anything. Now, if you have a big brother, he delights in teaching you what he knows. Randy would often share his roping wisdom with me, things like "Don't rope something you can't get loose from" and "Be sure your horse is big enough to hold what you catch."

Every day I would ask him, "Reckon you could teach me to rope better when I'm horseback?" His reply was always, "You need more groundwork. You need to be able to rope anything at any time. Be here, in front of the barn at first light tomorrow, and we'll see what your aim looks like."

I was as excited as a kid on Christmas Eve when I went to bed that night. When I heard that old Dominique rooster crow the next morning, I was down the stairs and out the door with my rope in hand. As I stood there in the dawn's early glow, I thought to myself, *Today I'm going to become a super looper! Nothing is out there that I can't snare with my trusty lasso.*

When Randy got there, he told me that the first thing we needed to do was to work on my strength and stamina, because it takes a lot of muscle to swing a rope all day. So first we filled up the feed buckets, and I carried them to feed the horses. Then I scooped cow feed for Daddy's old milk cows into a wheelbarrow all while Randy sat on a bale of hay, shouting, "Make sure you get it full; that way you won't have to make two trips."

As an eight-year-old boy, it took nearly all I had to lift up that steel-wheeled wheelbarrow with a hundred pounds of feed. As I pushed the barrow,

---

* *Houlihan:* a one-swing flip shot at a calf traveling in front of you from left to right.

Randy was nice enough to open the gate for me. Then I scooped the feed into all three troughs and headed back to the barn. I thought surely my muscles had had enough working to move on to roping. By the time I got all Randy's chores done, it was breakfast time, and roping lessons had been postponed. Disappointed, I told Randy, "You said we was going to rope, what's the deal?" He replied, "A feller has to have his groceries if he is going to rope all day. I promise right after we eat, the lessons will start again."

Shortly after breakfast, we were working on my loop size and swinging. "You have to be ready," Randy instructed. "Too much swinging and your arm will tire out before you even throw the loop. It's like shooting a rifle: Aim and fire." He had me stand with my back to the roping dummy, a practice tool that we'd constructed out of a wooden sawhorse with a 2 × 4-foot block at the end of it. He instructed me that when he hollered

ready, I would turn around, swing my loop one time, and throw it. I was surprised to see with practice over and over how many times I roped that wooden block. After about fifteen minutes, Randy said, "Now you need to be able to rope a moving target as it comes by. Turn your back and when I say *go*, turn around fast as you can and swing that loop and throw it at whatever is coming by."

Why I didn't ask Randy what was going to be coming by, I really don't know, but I was too focused on my roping skills at the time to ask questions. When I heard him holler *go*, I turned around and saw Randy herding an old rooster we had toward me. Before we go any further, let me give you a little background on this rooster and me. We didn't have a good relationship. He had chased me out of the chicken pen, flogged me with his spurs, and pecked my ankles until they bled. I was scared of him, and he knew it.

So, when I turned and saw the rooster, my instinct and practice got ahead of my courage, and the loop was on its way. My aim was on the money!

Randy was hollering, "You got him now, little brother! Now what are you going to do with him?" If I had been smart, I would've just dropped the rope and run for cover, but it all happened so fast, and I didn't know a rooster could climb up a rope that fast! He was on top of me before I knew what had happened. I was down on my back and had my arms wrapped across my face as feathers were flying. All I could hear was Randy laughing, and it was right then that I remembered one of his first rules of roping: Don't rope something you can't turn loose.

I rolled over and scrambled for the barn as fast as I could, rope still in hand, and the rooster in hot pursuit. When I rounded the corner of the barn, heading to the feed room, is when it happened. A dragging rope is just looking for something to hang on, and I was so glad it did. As I ran through the door of the feed room, the rope caught the crack of the door . . . and justice finally had been served. I hung me a rooster, and a mean one at that.

Mama had been hearing all the commotion from the house and came out to find me with my face bleeding and a dead rooster with a rope around its neck. She knew better than to ask. She just smiled and said, "You caught it, you clean it, and Randy can help you."

As Randy and I went about our task of cleaning the rooster, I asked him, "Randy, am I a super looper now?" He grinned and said, "For sure, little brother, you're the first cowboy I know that has roped supper!"

There's something about a beer batter that takes fried food to another level. The carbonation of the beer along with the cornstarch and baking powder allow the batter to fluff up while cooking and also give it crispness. Just a little garlic powder, seasoned salt, and pepper give this all the flavoring the batter needs. I like to use a light beer, but you can also substitute for a darker lager, if you enjoy the taste.

BEER-BATTERED FISH AND CHIPS

MAKES 4 TO 6 SERVINGS

PREP TIME: 20 MINUTES

TOTAL TIME: 40 MINUTES

4 russet potatoes

4 (4-ounce) white fish fillets, such as cod, catfish, or halibut

1 cup all-purpose flour

⅓ cup cornstarch, plus more for dusting

4 teaspoons baking powder

½ tablespoon garlic powder

½ tablespoon seasoned salt

½ tablespoon black pepper

1 (16-ounce) can light beer

Oil, for frying

Tartar sauce and ketchup, for serving

1. Rinse and slice the potatoes into thin fries. Place the cut potatoes in a large bowl and cover with cool water. Swirl the potatoes around, then drain the water. Repeat until the water is clear. Drain one last time, then transfer to a towel and pat dry. Set aside.

2. Slice each fillet into 4 even strips to ensure an even frying time. Pat dry with paper towels and set aside.

3. In a large bowl, combine the flour, ⅓ cup cornstarch, baking powder, garlic powder, seasoned salt, and pepper. Pour in 12 ounces of the beer and whisk until smooth. Add a little more beer, if needed, to achieve a pancake batter consistency.

4. In a large saucepan or Dutch oven, heat about 3 inches of oil to 350°F. Preheat the oven to 170° to 200°F. Place a wire rack on a large baking sheet and set aside.

5. Dust the fillets lightly with cornstarch to help the batter stick to the fish. Working in batches, dip the fillets in the wet mixture and then carefully place in the hot oil, a few at a time. Fry until both sides are golden brown, 3 to 4 minutes. Place on the prepared baking sheet in the oven to keep warm while you fry the remaining potatoes.

6. Add 2 to 4 ounces of the remaining beer into the batter mixture, mixing well, until it reaches a thinner pancake batter consistency. Dip the potatoes into the batter to thoroughly coat. Carefully add the potatoes, a few at a time, to the hot oil and fry until all sides are golden brown, 3 to 4 minutes. Place on a wire rack.

7. Serve fish and chips warm with tartar sauce and ketchup on the side.

A good tuna sandwich is one thing. A good grilled cheese is another. Now, when you combine the two . . . you are onto some cheesy goodness! We are kicking this up a notch and creating some of the best tuna you ever did taste. Go ahead and use the tuna base for this anytime you are making a regular sandwich, because the addition of the capers and horseradish pair really well with the fish and give it a good tangy flavor. Pile this up on a thick-cut piece of sourdough with melted cheese and you've got a meal.

TANGY TUNA MELT

MAKES 2 SANDWICHES

PREP TIME: 5 MINUTES

TOTAL TIME: 25 MINUTES

2 (4-ounce) cans solid white albacore tuna packed in water, drained

2 heaping tablespoons mayonnaise

½ to 1 tablespoon prepared horseradish

1 to 2 tablespoons Worcestershire sauce

¼ cup chopped green onion

2 tablespoons sweet relish

1 tablespoon capers

Salt and black pepper

Softened butter, for spreading

4 slices thick-cut sourdough bread

4 tablespoons shredded Parmesan cheese

4 tablespoons shredded cheddar cheese

4 tablespoons shredded mozzarella cheese

1. In a medium bowl, combine the tuna, mayonnaise, horseradish, Worcestershire sauce, green onion, relish, and capers. Season with salt and pepper to taste. Adjust any of the ingredients to taste, if desired. Cover and set aside.

2. Preheat a large cast-iron skillet over medium heat.

3. Generously spread butter on both sides of the bread slices. Place the bread in the skillet and toast until about halfway toasted. Flip over and sprinkle the slices with about 1 tablespoon of Parmesan cheese. Continue cooking until the opposite side is about halfway toasted. Remove from the skillet.

4. Sprinkle both partially toasted bread slices with about 2 tablespoons of cheddar cheese. Top each slice with about half of the tuna mixture followed by about 2 tablespoons of mozzarella cheese. Top each sandwich with the remaining bread slices.

5. Return the sandwiches to the skillet and cook until golden brown and crispy. Flip and slightly mash the sandwich down with a spatula and cook until golden brown and crispy. Don't be afraid to flip several times to achieve the desired color. Serve immediately.

This ain't just a sandwich—this is a bite of history. It's been claimed that this sandwich was coined in New Orleans in the late 1920s during a streetcar worker strike and was served for free to the strikers. Another story claims that this was made for local farmers, dock workers, and other "poor boys." Whatever the tradition, I'm glad it made it to our camp. Perfectly fried-up shrimp and a jazzed-up coleslaw mixed with the bold flavor of a chipotle mayonnaise sauce. Let's all go down to the Bayou!

SHRIMP PO' BOY

MAKES 4 SANDWICHES

PREP TIME: 1 HOUR

TOTAL TIME: 1 HOUR AND 15 MINUTES

1 cup mayonnaise

3 to 4 chipotle chiles in adobo sauce, chopped

4 garlic cloves, minced

4 to 5 tablespoons red wine vinegar

1½ tablespoons sugar

½ tablespoon lemon juice

1 (16-ounce) bag coleslaw

1½ cups buttermilk

2 teaspoons smoked paprika

2 tablespoons hot sauce

1 tablespoon baking powder

1 cup all-purpose flour

2 cups yellow cornmeal

2 tablespoons cornstarch

½ tablespoon garlic powder

½ tablespoon seasoned salt

½ tablespoon black pepper

20 large raw red or rock shrimp, peeled and deveined

Oil, for frying

4 hoagie buns

1. In a medium bowl, whisk together the mayonnaise, chipotle chiles, garlic, vinegar, sugar, and lemon juice.

2. Place the coleslaw mix in a large bowl. Stir in about one-half to one-third of the mayonnaise sauce, coating the slaw well. Note: The mixture will become juicier as it sits, but you can add more sauce later if it's too dry. Cover and place in the fridge for at least 1 hour before serving.

3. Meanwhile, in another medium bowl, whisk together the buttermilk, paprika, hot sauce, and baking powder.

4. In a large bowl, combine the flour, cornmeal, cornstarch, garlic powder, seasoned salt, and pepper.

5. Dip the shrimp in the wet mixture and then dredge through the flour mixture. Repeat to double coat. Place on a wire rack and repeat with the remaining shrimp. Place the shrimp in the fridge for 15 minutes to help the coating adhere better.

6. In a large saucepan or Dutch oven, heat about 3 inches of oil to 350°F. Working in batches, carefully add the shrimp, a few at a time, to the hot oil and fry until golden brown, 3 to 4 minutes. Remove with a slotted spoon and transfer to a wire rack or paper towels to cool slightly and drain. Repeat with the remaining shrimp.

7. Slice the rolls in half lengthwise. Place 5 shrimp down the center of each bun. Top with some coleslaw and a drizzle of the remaining mayonnaise sauce. Serve immediately.

There is no telling how many times Shannon and I have gone through the drive-up window at McDonald's and ordered the Big Mac while traveling on the road to different events. Believe me, it's hard to maneuver a truck and a twenty-eight-foot trailer hauling a chuck wagon through the drive-thru. We wanted to cowboy-up this iconic American burger, and it's gotten more than five million views on our YouTube channel and still counting. It's about the beef, because we're adding a generous pound per burger. We've also created a special sauce but added a little smoky flavor with adobo peppers, garlic powder, and sweet relish.

DRIVE-UP DOUBLE CHEESEBURGER WITH SPECIAL SAUCE

MAKES 2 HAMBURGERS

PREP TIME: 5 MINUTES
TOTAL TIME: 20 MINUTES

2 pounds 80% lean ground beef
Salt and black pepper

4 sesame seed buns
Softened butter, for spreading
Special Sauce (recipe follows)
½ to 1 cup finely chopped lettuce

4 slices cheddar cheese
Sliced pickles, for topping

1. Preheat a large cast-iron skillet over medium heat.

2. Form the beef into 4 equal-size patties and indent the middles slightly. Sprinkle both sides of the patties with salt and pepper.

3. In the heated skillet over medium heat, cook the patties for 3 minutes per side, or until at least medium to medium-well done. Remove from the skillet. Set aside and keep warm.

4. Take one of the top buns and cut off the top fourth (this will make the middle bun for the double-decker burger). Discard the seeded top.

5. Take the top buns, bottom buns, and the 2 cut buns and butter the insides. Return to the skillet and toast. Be sure to toast both sides of the cut bun.

6. Spread a layer of the sauce on one of the bottom buns and top with some lettuce, 1 slice of the cheese, a burger patty, and the cut bun. Spread another layer of sauce on top followed by more lettuce, a second slice of cheese, and a second burger patty. Top with pickles and the top bun. Repeat with the remaining ingredients to assemble the other cheeseburger. Serve immediately.

SPECIAL SAUCE

MAKES ABOUT 1 CUP

PREP TIME: 5 MINUTES

TOTAL TIME: 1 HOUR AND 5 MINUTES

½ cup mayonnaise

2 tablespoons sweet relish

1½ tablespoons mustard

1 tablespoon adobo sauce

1½ tablespoons apple cider vinegar

2 teaspoons sugar

½ teaspoon garlic powder

1 teaspoon onion powder

1 teaspoon smoked paprika

½ white onion, diced

In a medium mixing bowl, whisk together all the ingredients. Cover and place in the fridge for at least 1 hour before serving.

I know you've seen those Hungry Man dinners at your local grocery store in the frozen food aisle. I know homemade is best, but sometimes you just want a quick meal, and after a long day of feeding cows in the cold, I'd slap one of these in the microwave and it was nearly like Mama making a meal. But now we're doing it homemade with good ground beef sautéed in a rich, thick mushroom gravy. Be sure you make the Best Mashed Taters (page 142) to complete this meal.

HUNGRY COWBOY SALISBURY STEAK

MAKES 6 SERVINGS

PREP TIME: 30 MINUTES
TOTAL TIME: 45 MINUTES

1½ pounds 80% lean ground beef
4 tablespoons ketchup
3 tablespoons Worcestershire sauce
2 teaspoons dry mustard

2 teaspoons smoked paprika
1 teaspoon salt
1 teaspoon black pepper
2 large eggs, beaten
1¼ cups bread crumbs
4 tablespoons butter
1 tablespoon avocado oil or olive oil

1 white onion, diced
1 pound white button or cremini mushrooms, stemmed and sliced
6 tablespoons all-purpose flour
5 cups beef broth
2 tablespoons dry red wine

1. In a large bowl, use your hands to combine the ground beef, ketchup, 2 tablespoons of the Worcestershire sauce, the dry mustard, paprika, salt, pepper, and eggs. Slowly add the bread crumbs and continue hand-mixing until evenly combined. Cover and place in the fridge for at least 30 minutes.

2. Meanwhile, in a large cast-iron skillet over medium heat, melt 2 tablespoons of the butter with the oil. Toss in the onion and mushrooms and cook, stirring occasionally, until the onion is translucent and the mushrooms are golden brown, about 8 minutes.

3. Sprinkle in the flour and cook for about 3 minutes, stirring constantly. Reduce the heat to medium-low and stir in the beef broth, wine,

and the remaining 1 tablespoon Worcestershire sauce. Cook, stirring occasionally, until the gravy thickens, about 10 minutes. Transfer the contents to a large bowl and set aside.

4. Divide the beef mixture into 6 even pieces. Wet your hands with a little water and begin to shape them into ½-inch-thick oval patties.

5. In the same skillet over medium heat, melt the remaining 2 tablespoons butter. Add the beef patties and cook until golden brown on the outside, 2 to 3 minutes per side.

6. Pour the mushroom gravy over the meat and cook, stirring occasionally, until the meat is cooked through, 3 to 5 minutes. Serve warm.

My mother and I ate many microwavable potpies on Sunday evenings after church. I sure did enjoy them, but I have improved on this dish to give it a homemade flavor. Now, you could go ahead and substitute the meat with rotisserie chicken from the store, but let's add more flavor to that yard bird by smoking him! A generous topping of chicken, cream gravy, mushrooms, and carrots are piled high on top of our homemade pie crust. This will feed a crew, so y'all better come hungry.

CHICKEN POTPIE

MAKES ABOUT 8 SERVINGS

PREP TIME: 5 MINUTES
TOTAL TIME: 2 HOURS AND 10 MINUTES

1 (4- to 5-pound) whole chicken
Avocado oil or olive oil
Salt and black pepper
1 stick butter
2 yellow onions, chopped

3 large carrots, thinly sliced
8 ounces white button or cremini mushrooms, stemmed and sliced
6 garlic cloves, minced
1 cup all-purpose flour
2 cups chicken broth
¾ cup heavy cream

Leaves from 2 sprigs fresh thyme
1½ cups frozen corn
½ cup chopped fresh parsley
1 large egg
2 store-bought prerolled pie crusts, or 1 recipe Best Flaky Pie Crust (page 242), rolled out and unbaked

1. Clean, oil, and preheat the grill to 250°F. (See "Grate Care" on page 182.)

2. Spatchcock the chicken: Place the chicken on a cutting board breast side down. With a knife or scissors, cut the backbone out. Firmly press the chicken down to break the breastbone so it will lie flat. Clip the wing tips off and discard.

3. Pat the chicken down with paper towels to dry well. Generously rub with oil, then season well with salt and pepper.

4. Place the chicken on the indirect heat side of the grill. Cook for 1 to 1½ hours, until the internal temperature of the chicken is 165°F. Remove and let cool slightly before shredding or cutting into bite-size pieces.

5. Preheat the oven to 425°F.

6. In a large cast-iron skillet over medium heat, melt the butter. Stir in the onions and carrots. Cook for 8 minutes, or until the carrots are tender. Stir in the mushrooms and cook for 5 minutes, or until the mushrooms are tender. Add the garlic and stir.

7. Sprinkle in the flour and mix well. Cook for 2 to 3 minutes, stirring constantly.

8. Pour in the broth and cream. Add the thyme. Simmer, stirring occasionally, until the mixture thickens, 2 to 3 minutes. Season with salt and pepper.

9. Stir in the shredded chicken, corn, and parsley. Remove from the heat and set aside.

10. In a small bowl, whisk together the egg with 2 tablespoons water.

11. Place 1 rolled-out pie crust dough in a 12-inch cast-iron skillet and top with the chicken mixture. Top with the remaining crust and cut several vent holes. Brush the egg wash on top of the crust.

12. Bake until the crust is golden brown, 30 to 35 minutes. Cut and serve warm.

I know you're thinking to yourself, *What's so hard about making a mashed potato?* Well, folks, there's nothing hard about it, but there are a few tricks I'm sharing to ensure you get the *best* mashed taters. Use a blend of russet and Yukon Gold to get a hearty potato along with one that blends up creamy. Be sure to let the steam escape after boiling the potatoes so they aren't too soggy. Finally blend them up well with a mixture of cream cheese and butter for extra creaminess.

BEST MASHED TATERS

MAKES 6 TO 8 SERVINGS

PREP TIME: 5 MINUTES

TOTAL TIME: 20 MINUTES

2 pounds russet potatoes, peeled

2 pounds Yukon Gold potatoes, peeled

1 to 1½ cups half-and-half

6 tablespoons butter

3 garlic cloves, minced

6 ounces cream cheese, softened

Coarsely ground salt and black pepper

Chopped green onions, for topping (optional)

1. Cut the potatoes into equal-size pieces and place in a large stockpot. Add just enough water to cover the potatoes by about 1 inch. Bring to a boil for 10 minutes, or until they are fork tender. Be careful not to overcook the potatoes or they will become mushy.

2. Meanwhile, place the half-and-half, butter, and garlic in a small pot over medium-low heat. Cook, stirring occasionally, until the butter melts and the mixture has warmed through. Set aside.

3. Drain the water from the potatoes. Place the potatoes in the stockpot over low heat to let all the steam and moisture evaporate.

4. Remove from the heat. Add the cream cheese to the potatoes and mash together with a potato masher.

5. Pour in half of the half-and-half mixture and continue mashing (or blend with a mixer). Gradually mix in the remaining half-and-half mixture until you reach the desired consistency. Season with salt and pepper to taste and, if using, top with green onions.

JUST KEEP GOING

I've been down a lot of roads in my life, especially on the seat of a wagon. Some rough, some smooth, and all of them different. From four-wheel drive to four-legged, it seemed that when I finally got to my destination, it was all worth the effort and humps in the road.

The first time that I ever cooked in the Palo Duro Canyon was in November 1998. We were camping for three weeks in some mighty rough country. The crew was new to me and the country was too. We were going to pull our trailers into camp from the Plains Corral to Summerfield Park. As a crow flies, it was probably around six miles, but on the winding pasture roads it was more like twelve miles. Before leaving, the boss man told me, "Just follow the remuda into camp, you won't have no trouble."

Now, for those of y'all that aren't cavvy savvy (*cavvy* is another term used in the West for remuda), the remuda is the band of horses that belongs to each cowboy. Typically for a three-week works, each cowboy would have three or four horses, so the remuda made up about forty or so horses.

The boss man continued, "You're going to go through three gates, just keep going. When you get to the last one, there is a road that goes off to the right. Don't take it—just keep going till you see that windmill and then go left. Right after that you're going to go down a long, steep hill, and when you get to the bottom, go right. Go down about two hundred yards and you will see an old cedar tree with most of the limbs gone.

Don't pay it any mind, just keep going until you see that big woodpile. That is camp."

As he walked off, I thought to myself, *He must have never worked for Rand McNally!* I don't think I ever saw any directions on one of their maps that said "just keep going." The directions he gave me were ones that needed to come with a tour guide and compass.

I wasn't traveling on a maintained dirt road. This was a pasture road that had been manicured by years of wind, heavy rain, and a lot of cow tracks. Outcroppings of rock and mesquite branches were the guardrails, and a divided highway here was when there was a cedar tree right in the middle of the road. I didn't have to worry about a speed limit either, because the only time I might get above ten mph is if the brakes quit working on the trailer going downhill. The gullies along the sides of the road were knee deep to a tall giraffe and the switchbacks so sharp you could check the air pressure in the rear tires on the trailer just by rolling down the window. And where were my lovely trail guides? Those horses that were supposed to be leading the way were out of sight before I had time to start the pickup truck. I was having to track them at every gate and crossroad just to make sure I was headed in the right direction.

I had just pulled through my third gate when I thought to myself, *I've been going down this pasture road for nearly an hour now. And that bare cedar tree he was telling me to look out for . . . well, that's nearly every other tree.* I was wondering if anyone around here had heard of a road sign, just something simple, like "Camp This Way" or "Don't worry, you ain't lost yet." *If I ever get there*, I thought, *you can sure bet I'm going to tie a flag on the tallest point I can find, and I might even put a flashlight on it too.*

I don't know if it was luck or if I was a good tracker, but after about twenty more minutes, I rounded a corner and there was a woodpile big enough to last three months. I had made it to Summerfield Park.

I unloaded the wagon, set up the fly, and unloaded all my cooking gear. I commenced to cook supper as the rest of the hands got their teepees set up. Camp was finally coming together and looked like home.

After supper, the boss man said, "You reckon you could bring dinner to a set of pens up top? That way we could keep working." What he meant by "up top" was at the top layer of the caprock. We were camped on the third level.

"Is it back up that same road?" I asked.

"Yep, right where we started from," he said.

Bedtime came early and so did breakfast. It was around 6 a.m. when the cowboys went to saddle their horses. There wouldn't be much downtime this morning, because I figured I would need to start lunch soon to give myself enough time to travel all the way back up to the pens. Being as it was a cold and windy day, I made a good

traditional chuck wagon trail stew loaded with potatoes and chunked beef to keep them full and warm. I also cooked up two Dutch ovens full of corn bread.

I had everything loaded up, when I remembered I had some fluorescent flagging tape in my duffel bag. I was going to mark this trail better than Lewis and Clark! So, at every corner, I tied a three-foot piece of tape to a cedar bush or mesquite tree limb. It took me nearly two hours to make the journey to the pens that day, but a good hour of that was flagging and opening gates.

Later that afternoon when the boys got back into camp, laughing, they asked, "Did you see anyone doing some surveying on your way in or out? They sure hung a lot of flagging!" I just grinned and said, "Yep, the highway crew came by, and they got it all marked off. They said they'd start paving tomorrow."

I ended up cooking for this outfit for the next twelve years. As the years went by, the flagging slowly disappeared due to wind and weather. The roads got a little better, as did my memory on where I was and how to get to where I was going. It's been nearly twenty years since I was in that country, but if I ever go back, I'm going to put up a road sign for a cook in the future that reads, "Just keep going . . . it is just around some corner, somewhere."

SWEATERS, 'STACHES, AND SOUP OF THE DAY
SOUPS AND STEWS

Since we are on the subject of soup, I can remember being in Brandon, Manitoba, one year in December to entertain for a cowboy Christmas Ball. Now, I'm familiar with winter. It's that time of year when a first-year heifer will always decide to have her calf right in the middle of a snowstorm. I thought I had winter pretty much figured out, but those good Canadians showed me they put a whole new twist on the word *winter*.

When I landed in Winnipeg, it was a toasty −27°F. During the brisk walk from the terminal to the rental car, my mustache had frozen solid. Reminded me of the time I was horseback along the Red River in Oklahoma, checking wheat pasture cattle in December. I was out riding for about two hours, and I didn't have anything covering my face. By the time I got done, there were ice crystals covering my mustache and the ends had broken off. I just thought of it as a free haircut courtesy of Mother Nature. I drove the two hours to my motel room and nestled in for the night. It was a short night that followed, and I was up by 5 a.m. and looking for some coffee and eggs. Across the road, I saw a diner with a parking lot full of ranch trucks. The paint was half gone on most of them and the back ends were full of feed sacks. Looked like my kind of crowd, so I headed over.

As I entered the door, it was as if someone had announced, "Here comes the Okie," and they all gave me that "you aren't from around here" look. Our hats were shaped differently and our facial hair sure was different. All the men had those big lamb chop–looking sideburns that wrapped from their ears along their jawline and to the edge of their mouths. And while I was layered in every piece of clothing I packed in the suitcase, they looked as if they were outfitted for a spring morning with a light sweater.

I made my way back to the corner booth, hung my hat on the wall, and sat down. My waitress asked, "Can I get you started with some coffee and our soup of the day?"

"Soup, ma'am?" I answered. "It's five in the morning. I ain't never had soup for breakfast. Did y'all run out of bacon and eggs?" She just grinned and said she'd bring me a coffee. As I surveyed the diner, I did notice everyone had a coffee and a bowl of soup. I thought I must be missing out on something and figured when in Rome . . . Maybe they were hiding the bacon in the soup.

When the waitress brought me the coffee, I asked her if she minded bringing me a cup of that soup of the day. When I got the soup, it was mostly broth with a few veggies. If you did some deep-sea fishing, you could also find a little meat in there.

By this time, most of the regulars were heading out, all except an old feller dressed in Levi's, a wool vest, and an earflap cap. He shuffled over to my booth and said, "Excuse me, you're not from these parts, are you?"

"What gave the secret away?" I asked.

He laughed and said, "Well, we could tell by your dress and noticeable lack of facial whiskers. You must be from south of here."

"Yep," I answered, "just about fifteen hundred miles south."

"We hope you enjoy your stay here, and if you can drop in again, we'll buy your supper."

"Does it come with the soup of the day?" I asked.

He grinned and replied, "Every day, all day, all year. Different bowls, same soup, but it'll warm you up and there's usually good company to go with it."

> "... it'll warm you up and there's usually good company to go with it."

Not only is this a ranch favorite, but it's also one of my family's favorites too. This is a hearty and more soup-like version of a Hamburger Helper. Some of you may even know it as "slumgullion." This is an easy throw-together meal of ground beef, canned tomatoes (Ro-Tel brand for extra flavor), and lots of noodles. It's perfect for feeding the family on a busy weekday night.

AMERICAN-STYLE GOULASH

MAKES 6 SERVINGS

PREP TIME: 10 MINUTES

TOTAL TIME: 50 MINUTES

2 pounds ground beef

1 large yellow onion, chopped

1 tablespoon smoked paprika

3 cloves garlic, minced

1 (15-ounce) can stewed tomatoes

1 (14.5-ounce) can diced tomatoes, undrained

1 (6-ounce) can tomato paste

1 (10-ounce) can diced tomatoes and green chiles

1 cup chicken broth

2 tablespoons soy sauce

2 bay leaves

1 Anaheim or green chile, roasted and peeled, or 1 (4-ounce) can diced green chiles

2 cups uncooked large elbow macaroni

Salt and black pepper

1. In a large cast-iron skillet over medium-high heat, cook the ground beef until it begins to brown, about 4 minutes. Stir in the onion and continue cooking until the meat has browned, another minute or so. Drain the grease and discard.

2. Place the beef and onion mixture in a stew pot over medium heat. Stir in the paprika, garlic, stewed tomatoes, diced tomatoes, tomato paste, diced tomatoes and green chiles, broth, ½ cup water, soy sauce, bay leaves, and Anaheim chile. Cover and reduce the heat to a simmer for 20 minutes.

3. Stir in the macaroni and continue to simmer, covered, stirring occasionally until the pasta is tender, about 20 minutes. Be careful not to overcook the noodles. Remove and discard the bay leaves. Season with salt and pepper to taste. Serve warm.

Don't let this fancy French name scare you off, because this is just our version of a beef stew in red wine made famous by Julia Child. I do believe she would approve of my cowboy version of this classic. Be sure to start with chuck roast instead of stew meat, which will give you a more tender cut. The beef cooks down in a rich red wine broth with mushrooms, pearl onions, and carrots. I like to serve this over mashed potatoes, and as Julia would say, "Bon appétit!"

BEEF BOURGUIGNON
BEEF STEW IN RED WINE

MAKES 6 TO 8 SERVINGS

PREP TIME: 35 MINUTES

TOTAL TIME: 2 HOURS AND 20 MINUTES

1 (4-pound) chuck roast, cut into 1-inch chunks

Salt and black pepper

3 tablespoons olive oil

1 (750-ml) bottle dry red wine

8 slices bacon, roughly chopped

1 pound frozen pearl onions

2 white onions, roughly chopped

4 large carrots, sliced into 1-inch pieces (about 2 cups)

4 garlic cloves, minced

3 to 4 cups beef broth

2 teaspoons dried thyme

2 tablespoons tomato paste

4 tablespoons unsalted butter

1 pound white button or cremini mushrooms, stemmed and sliced

3 tablespoons all-purpose flour

Mashed potatoes or garlic bread, for serving (optional)

1. Preheat the oven to 350°F.

2. Pat the meat dry with paper towels. Generously season all sides with salt and pepper.

3. In a large cast-iron skillet over medium-high heat, heat 1 tablespoon of the olive oil. Add half of the meat to the skillet and cook until browned on all sides, about 8 minutes. Transfer the meat to a 12-inch Dutch oven or large oven-safe pot with a lid. Add 1 tablespoon of the olive oil to the skillet and repeat with the remaining meat.

4. Pour ¼ cup of the wine in the hot skillet to deglaze. Stir around the pan and scrape the contents into the Dutch oven.

5. Place the bacon in the skillet and cook over medium-high heat, stirring occasionally, just until browned, about 5 minutes. Strain the bacon from the pan, leaving any grease in the skillet, and add the bacon to the pot. Stir in the pearl onions.

6. Add the white onions and carrots to the skillet and cook in the bacon grease over medium heat, stirring occasionally, until the onions begin to brown, about 5 minutes.

7. Stir in the garlic and continue cooking for another minute, stirring constantly. Stir the contents of the skillet into the pot.

8. Pour the remaining wine in the pot. Add enough broth to just cover the meat and vegetables. Stir in the thyme and tomato paste.

9. Place the Dutch oven over medium-high heat and bring the stew to a good simmer. Cover and transfer to the oven. Cook for 1½ hours, or until the meat is fork tender.

10. About 10 minutes before the stew is done, in a large skillet over medium heat, melt 2 tablespoons of the butter with the remaining 1 tablespoon olive oil. Stir in the mushrooms and cook for 5 minutes, or until they begin to brown.

11. Slowly mix in the flour and the remaining 2 tablespoons of butter. Stir the mushrooms constantly until the flour is absorbed. Remove the Dutch oven from the oven and stir in the mushrooms.

12. Place the Dutch oven over medium-high heat and bring to a simmer, uncovered, for about 15 minutes, to let the mixture thicken slightly. Serve on top of mashed potatoes or with garlic bread, if desired.

Folks, forget the canned stuff, 'cause this recipe comes with homemade egg noodles. That may sound a little intimidating, but these noodles are easier to make than you think and make all the difference in the texture and the flavor of this soup.

CHICKEN SOUP WITH HOMEMADE EGG NOODLES

MAKES ABOUT 6 SERVINGS

PREP TIME: 5 MINUTES

TOTAL TIME: 1 HOUR AND 30 MINUTES

2 large skinless, boneless chicken breasts or thighs

4 tablespoons butter

4 (14.5-ounce) cans chicken broth

1 white onion, chopped

1 cup chopped celery

1 cup thinly sliced carrots

2 garlic cloves, minced

2 teaspoons dried sage

2 teaspoons poultry seasoning

Egg Noodles (recipe follows)

Salt and black pepper

1. Place 4 cups water in a medium stockpot over medium-high heat.

2. Add the chicken and 2 tablespoons of the butter. Cover and bring to a boil for 30 to 45 minutes, until the chicken is fork tender.

3. Remove the chicken to cool and reserve the cooking water. When cool enough to handle, shred or chop the chicken into bite-size pieces.

4. Stir the chicken back into the pot with the water. Add the broth, onion, celery, carrots, garlic, sage, poultry seasoning, and the remaining 2 tablespoons butter. Bring to a boil for 15 to 20 minutes, until the carrots are tender.

5. Stir the noodles into the pot and reduce the heat to medium-low. Let simmer for 15 to 20 minutes, until the noodles are tender. Be careful not to undercook the noodles or they will be gummy. Season with salt and pepper to taste and serve warm.

EGG NOODLES

MAKES ABOUT 6 SERVINGS

PREP TIME: 10 MINUTES

TOTAL TIME: 25 MINUTES

1¼ cups all-purpose flour, plus more for dusting

2 teaspoons poultry seasoning

½ teaspoon salt

2 tablespoons butter, softened

¼ cup milk

1 egg, beaten

1. In a medium bowl, combine the flour, poultry seasoning, and salt. Cut the butter in with a fork until crumbly.

2. Stir in the milk and egg. Lightly work the dough with your hands until it forms a soft ball. You may need to add a little more milk or flour to achieve the desired consistency.

3. Cover and let sit for 5 minutes.

4. Turn the dough out onto a floured surface. Roll out to about ⅛ inch thick. Cut the noodles into strips. Separate and let rest for about 15 minutes to allow the noodles to dry out a bit, which will help them keep their shape when cooking.

PROVISIONS THEN AND NOW

THEN . . .

The height of the cattle drive days happened in the 1860s to the late 1880s, when cowboys would herd fifteen hundred to three thousand head of cattle up north. A typical crew was eight to twelve men and a cook. To feed these cowboys, the chuck wagon was used as a mobile kitchen. Breakfast and supper were typically the day's only meals and consisted of an extremely limited variety of beans, coffee, biscuits, and dried meat.

Breakfast would be served and then camp would be loaded up. The cook would drive the wagon ahead of the herd, so he could set up camp and get supper ready before the cowboys arrived. A fifteen-mile journey was typical for a day's ride. Supper would be had, and the whole process would start over again.

As the trails progressed and more stations set up along the way, goods and food preservation helped make for improved eating conditions down the trail. The wagon would be packed with as many food items and tools that could be carried and would be restocked with food along the way. But don't get the idea that there was a Walmart located every ten miles!

From a journal by XIT trail boss Ealey Moore, the following provisions were recorded for a crew of ten men during a thirteen-week drive from Channing, Texas, to Miles City, Montana, in 1892.*

160 pounds rice	1,750 pounds flour	Vanilla extract
160 pounds beans	405 pounds sugar	Cinnamon
9 gallons sorghum	720 pounds potatoes	Mustard
300 pounds fruit (dried currants, prunes, canned apples and peaches)	900 pounds bacon	Baking powder
	180 pounds coffee beans	Baking soda
	Pickle kegs	

Other common supplies found on a typical chuck wagon also included:

Salt pork	Sourdough starter	Lard
Salt	Dried chiles	
Onions	Garlic	

* Courtesy of Montana Historical Society.

HEREFORD CATTLE AND COWBOYS TAKING IT EASY AT A WATER HOLE IN THE PANHANDLE
With slight variations this scene is duplicated many times each day in Texas

Now . . .

Even though times have changed, there are a lot of similarities between the cookie back then and my job as a chuck wagon cook now. The cooking methods are still the same. Neither of us had fancy electric gadgets or knobs on an oven. All cooking is done with fire, whether grilling or with coals for Dutch-oven baking. However, the difference now is that I have a whole lot more to work with than he did back in the 1800s.

Because of trucking, there is no need to drive cattle hundreds of miles; instead, they are bought and sold locally or at regional markets and trucked out to their final destinations. There is still a need for cowboys to work cattle, and the main events happen during the spring and the fall. In the spring, the main tasks are vaccinating, branding, ear tagging, and castrating. Fall tasks include ear tagging, weaning, worming, and branding any of the herd, including calves, that were missed in the spring.

As a cook, my job is to feed cowboys during these times. But, for me, it's about not only keeping them fed but also making them feel comfortable during the long weeks of work. I've cooked out anywhere from five days to six weeks on a ranch. Depending on the size of the ranch, we will either set up camp in a single location, or we will pack up and move camp as the cowboys work different pastures or traps on the ranch. I cooked for one ranch where we moved camp every day for three weeks and drove the wagon 7 miles to the next camp. On the largest ranch I've cooked for, we moved camp about every three to four days and put over 160 miles on the wagon.

Another advantage I have over the cooks of the 1800s is food storage and preservation. I make a set menu for the time we will be cooking, which includes a majority of canned and dry goods. A few fresh fruits and vegetables will be on the list, but they are typically used at the beginning of the works, so as not to spoil. Instead of fresh vegetables, we often use frozen, because they'll keep better. Milk is on the list, but so is canned milk, and the sourdough starter we keep on the wagon also can substitute for milk in baking.

Cold foods are kept in YETI chests packed in ice. We will have separate coolers for meat, dairy, fruits/veggies, and extra ice. We reload on ice and any extra groceries every few days when a cowboy goes back to headquarters to stock up on supplies.

While on the trail, they may have only had two meals a day, we cook three hearty meals to keep those boys' energy up. Working cattle can typically burn anywhere from two hundred to four hundred calories per hour, and those boys put in a lot of hours.

On days we are moving camp, the lunch meal is a grab-and-go—a sandwich or burrito, anything they can stick in their pocket and eat along the way. We will then set up camp at the next location and prepare supper.

Here is an example of our grocery list for a five-week works for twelve cowboys:

Dry goods

20 pounds yellow cornmeal

40 pounds sugar

12 pounds coffee

50 pounds flour

3 sacks light brown sugar

7 pounds dry pinto beans

13 loaves bread

7 pounds rice

4 packages pasta

7 cans bread crumbs

4 blocks Velveeta

Chocolate chips

2 sacks powdered sugar

Assorted dried chiles

Canned goods

4 cartons beef broth

Lemon-lime soda

20 cans yellow hominy

30 cans green chiles

15 cans Ro-Tel diced tomatoes and green chiles

10 cans pork and beans

10 cans ranch-style beans

15 cans evaporated milk

14 cans tomato sauce

15 cans black beans

15 cans cream of mushroom soup

12 cans cream of chicken soup

10 cans black-eyed peas

10 cans chipotle chiles in adobo sauce

15 gallons vegetable oil

4 cans peaches

2 cans blueberry pie filling

2 cans apple pie filling

6 cans cherry pie filling

Condiments

2 bottles honey

6 bottles ketchup

5 jars assorted jelly

3 bottles BBQ sauce

5 jars mayonnaise

4 jars relish

4 syrup bottles

3 bottles Worcestershire sauce

3 bottles mustard

Meat

60 pounds bacon

30 pounds sausage

81 steaks

83 pounds ground beef

95 chicken fried steaks

20 pounds assorted lunch meat

64 bone-in pork chops

5 pounds stew meat

Dairy

8 pints sour cream

1 gallon heavy cream

4 sacks shredded cheddar cheese

10 pounds butter

119 cheese slices

720 eggs

8 gallons milk

10 blocks cream cheese

Spices

Rosemary

Garlic

Cinnamon

Vanilla

Pepper

Olive oil

Baking powder

Dried cilantro

Baking soda

Lemon juice

Dry yeast

Nutmeg

Lime juice

Salt

Cocoa powder

Chili powder

Cumin

Oregano

Garlic powder

Celery salt

Lime juice

Cornstarch

Veggies/Fruit

400 potatoes

50 onions

40 jalapeños

20 bell peppers

10 poblano chiles

5 pounds frozen corn

4 pounds frozen strawberries

10 pounds frozen green beans

I will tell you the truth . . . I always thought if it was called chili, it had to be made with beef. Boy, was I wrong, because sometimes it's nice to change up the old routine. This thick and creamy chili is infused with the Mexican flavors of oregano, cumin, and green chiles. I'm throwing in some good Great Northern beans for more texture and a more filling spoonful.

WHITE CHICKEN CHILI

MAKES 6 TO 8 SERVINGS

PREP TIME: 20 MINUTES

TOTAL TIME: 1 HOUR AND 20 MINUTES

2 large skinless, boneless chicken breasts

Salt and black pepper

2 tablespoons avocado oil or olive oil

2 white onions, chopped

3 garlic cloves, minced

1 tablespoon lemon juice

1 (32-ounce) carton chicken broth

2 to 3 (4-ounce) cans diced green chiles

3 (15.5-ounce) cans Great Northern beans, drained and rinsed

3 teaspoons ground cumin

3 teaspoons dried oregano

1 to 2 tablespoons chili seasoning

1 teaspoon red pepper flakes

8 ounces cream cheese, softened

1. Generously season the chicken with salt and black pepper.

2. Heat 1 tablespoon of the oil in a large cast-iron skillet over medium-high heat. Add the chicken. Cover the skillet and cook for about 10 minutes, flipping the chicken once while cooking. Remove the lid, and continue cooking until the chicken has browned on both sides and has reached an internal temperature of 165°F. Remove and set aside to cool slightly, then shred or chop into bite-size pieces.

3. Place a Dutch oven or large stew pot over medium heat. Add the remaining 1 tablespoon oil and the onions. Cook, stirring occasionally, until the onions are tender, about 5 minutes.

4. Stir in the garlic, lemon juice, broth, green chiles, 2 cans of the beans, cumin, oregano, chili seasoning, red pepper flakes, and cream cheese. Stir frequently until the cream cheese has melted. Stir in the chicken.

5. Run the remaining 1 can beans through the blender or mash with a potato masher until smooth.

6. Stir the mashed beans into the chili. Reduce the heat to medium-low and cook for about 1 hour, stirring occasionally. Serve warm.

TIP For extra creaminess, stir in ½ to 1 cup of heavy cream in step 4.

This creamy soup has a similar taste to pumpkin but is sweeter and with a nuttier flavor. It pairs well with a touch of cinnamon, nutmeg, and curry to give it a classic autumn flavor. I like to top this soup with some seasoned croutons for a touch of crunch to balance out the smooth texture of the soup.

BUTTERNUT SQUASH SOUP

MAKES ABOUT 8 SERVINGS

PREP TIME: 10 MINUTES

TOTAL TIME: 1 HOUR AND 40 MINUTES

1 stick butter

3 tablespoons olive oil

2 cups chopped yellow onion

2 medium sweet potatoes, peeled and chopped

1 cup chopped carrots

1 red bell pepper, chopped

6 cups peeled and chopped butternut squash (about 4 pounds)

4 cups chicken broth

1 cup heavy cream

1 to 2 tablespoons light brown sugar

1 teaspoon curry powder

½ teaspoon ground nutmeg

½ teaspoon ground cinnamon

Salt and black pepper

Seasoned croutons, for serving (optional)

1. In a large Dutch oven or pot over medium heat, melt the butter. Stir in the olive oil.

2. Add the onion, sweet potatoes, carrots, bell pepper, and squash.

3. Cover and reduce the heat to medium-low. Cook for 45 minutes to 1 hour, stirring occasionally, until the vegetables are soft. Allowing the vegetables to cook down for a longer period of time, at a low heat, helps release their natural sweetness.

4. Stir in the broth, cover, and cook for an additional 15 minutes.

5. Pour the contents of the skillet into a blender. Add the cream, brown sugar, curry powder, nutmeg, and cinnamon. Blend until smooth.

6. Pour the contents of the blender back into the Dutch oven and simmer over medium heat for about 15 minutes, letting the flavors incorporate and the soup to warm through. Season with salt and pepper to taste. Serve warm, topped with croutons, if desired.

"Like my daddy always said—you might load the wagon before you hitch up the mules."

Once again, we are headed down to the Bayou to cook up a traditional gumbo, or what us Okies call Cajun stew—with a little inspiration from Justin Wilson, who was one of my greatest culinary inspirations. I enjoyed watching his Southern-style cooking every weekend on PBS, and he always had a good story to go along with whatever dish he was making. I have made some cowboy adjustments, adding white wine and our own Cowboy Cajun Spice mix. You can also use some chorizo for the sausage. Serve this over rice for some fine Southern-style dining.

COWBOY CAJUN GUMBO

MAKES 6 TO 8 SERVINGS

PREP TIME: 40 MINUTES

TOTAL TIME: 2 HOURS AND 20 MINUTES

½ cup bacon grease

1 cup all-purpose flour

1 white onion, chopped

1 green bell pepper, chopped

1 cup chopped celery

4 garlic cloves, minced

4 cups beef broth, warmed

1½ pounds andouille sausage, sliced

1 tablespoon hot sauce

3 bay leaves

1 tablespoon Cowboy Cajun Spice (recipe follows)

1 teaspoon dried thyme

2 cups white wine

2 pounds raw shrimp, peeled and deveined

2 tablespoons Worcestershire sauce

Cooked white rice, for serving (optional)

1. In a Dutch oven or large pot over medium heat, melt the bacon grease. Slowly sift in the flour and reduce the heat to low. Cook, whisking constantly, until it thickens and is a dark brown color, about 15 minutes.

2. Increase the heat to medium-low. Stir in the onion, bell pepper, celery, and garlic and continue cooking, stirring frequently, until the vegetables are tender, about 10 minutes.

3. Increase the heat to medium. Stir in the broth and cook for about 10 minutes.

4. Stir in the sausage, hot sauce, bay leaves, spice mix, and thyme. Continue cooking for about 1 hour, stirring occasionally.

5. Reduce the heat to medium-low. Stir in the wine, shrimp, and Worcestershire sauce and let the mixture simmer for 30 to 40 minutes. Remove the bay leaves and discard. Serve warm over rice, if desired.

COWBOY CAJUN SPICE

MAKES HEAPING ½ CUP

3 tablespoons smoked paprika

2 tablespoons sea salt

2 tablespoons garlic powder

1 tablespoon coarsely ground black pepper

1 tablespoon onion powder

1 tablespoon dried oregano

½ tablespoon cayenne pepper

½ tablespoon dried thyme

In a small bowl, mix together all the ingredients until combined.

TIP This recipe makes more than the gumbo calls for but can be stored in the pantry for 6 months and used for another batch. You can also use it in other recipes where you want to add some Cajun flavor.

You may want to double this recipe because it just gets better every time you reheat it. Start with kidney beans, and instead of using the typical ham hock or salt pork, we're searing up ham steak. This char on the ham will give this a flavor boost. Cook the rice in chicken broth instead of water for a more savory flavor.

RED BEANS AND RICE

MAKES 6 TO 8 SERVINGS

PREP TIME: 25 MINUTES

TOTAL TIME: 2 HOURS AND 25 MINUTES

1½ pounds ham steak

1 pound dried red kidney beans, rinsed

2 tablespoons butter

1 large white onion, minced

1 cup chopped celery

1 green bell pepper, diced

6 garlic cloves, minced

3 bay leaves

1 teaspoon dried thyme

2 tablespoons chopped fresh parsley

2 teaspoons coarsely ground black pepper

3 cups uncooked white rice

Chicken broth, for cooking the rice (optional)

1. Place the ham in a large cast-iron skillet over medium-high heat. Cook for 3 to 4 minutes per side, or until lightly charred. Set aside to cool, then cut into bite-size pieces.

2. Place the beans in a large pot and cover with about 2 inches of water. Bring the beans to a boil, stirring occasionally. Note: For a faster cook time, you can soak the beans in cold water for 45 minutes (or up to overnight, for higher elevations).

3. Meanwhile, in a medium cast-iron skillet over medium heat, melt the butter. Stir in the onion, celery, and bell pepper. Cook for about 5 minutes, or until the onion begins to soften. Stir in the garlic and cook for another 4 minutes, until the onion and pepper are tender.

4. Add the onion mixture, bay leaves, thyme, parsley, black pepper, and ham to the beans and stir. Reduce the heat to a low boil, cover, and cook, stirring occasionally, until the beans are tender, 1 to 2 hours. Cooking times will vary depending on your elevation and if the beans were soaked. Be sure to keep the beans covered with water as they cook. Add hot water as needed.

5. Cook the rice as directed on the package. For a better flavor, we substitute broth for the water, but it's up to you.

6. Remove the bay leaves from the beans and serve warm over rice.

You have all seen it at the grocery store, regular ol' cans of pork and beans. I don't know about y'all, but I always had trouble finding the pork in them. That's why this recipe is called *real*, because we're using a hearty pork roast so you don't have to dig around to try to find the meat. You can use any bean you prefer, but we recommend Anasazi beans. They are a red-and-white speckled bean that comes from the Colorado, New Mexico, and Arizona areas. To me, they have a slightly sweeter, nuttier taste than pinto beans.

THE *REAL* PORK AND BEANS

MAKES 10 TO 12 SERVINGS

PREP TIME: 2 HOURS AND 10 MINUTES
TOTAL TIME: 5 HOURS AND 40 MINUTES

2 tablespoons dry mustard

2 teaspoons chili powder

2 teaspoons smoked paprika

½ tablespoon coarsely ground salt

1 tablespoon black pepper

1 (4- to 5-pound) pork roast or pork butt

6 garlic cloves, halved

4 tablespoons butter, melted

2 tablespoons olive oil

2 (32-ounce) cartons chicken broth

2 pounds Anasazi beans

2 white onions, quartered

2 dried ancho chiles, crushed

1 jalapeño, stemmed, seeded, and chopped

Salt and black pepper

Corn bread or rice, for serving (optional)

1. Preheat the oven to 350°F.

2. In a small bowl, combine the dry mustard, chili powder, paprika, salt, and pepper.

3. Generously rub the seasoning mixture evenly over the pork roast to coat well. Cover and place in the fridge for 1½ hours. Remove from the fridge about 40 minutes before cooking to bring to room temperature.

4. Place the roast, fat side down, on a cutting board and, with a sharp knife, poke holes around the top side. Tuck the halved garlic cloves in the holes, making sure they are inserted deep enough to be covered by the meat.

5. Pour the butter and olive oil in a deep Dutch oven or large roasting pan with a lid. Pour in 1 cup of the chicken broth.

6. Place the roast, fat side down, in the Dutch oven or pan. Cover with the lid and cook for 3 hours, until the roast is fork tender.

7. After the roast has been cooking for 1 hour, pour the remaining broth and 6 cups water in a large stockpot over medium-high heat. Stir in the beans, onions, dried chiles, and jalapeño and bring to a boil. Reduce to a simmer and season with salt and pepper to taste.

8. Cover and cook for 2 to 2½ hours, or until the beans begin to get tender. Cooking time will vary depending on elevation.

9. Remove the roast from the oven and transfer to a clean cutting board. Debone and shred or chop the meat. Stir the shredded meat into the beans and simmer for 30 minutes. Serve warm with corn bread or over rice, if desired.

This was always on the menu at the wagon on cold days. Stew was a staple on an ol' chuck wagon, but the cook didn't have as much to work with as we do. A little dried meat or wild game and any veggies he could muster up was about it. This is an easy meal using canned beans, hominy, and Ro-Tel tomatoes and chiles for a traditional stew base along with generous chunks of chuck roast. It's cowboy approved, and you can now enjoy it on the modern trail.

CHUCK WAGON TRAIL STEW

MAKES 8 TO 10 SERVINGS

PREP TIME: 30 MINUTES
TOTAL TIME: 2 HOURS

1 pound bacon, cut into 1-inch strips

2½ to 3 pounds chuck roast, trimmed and cubed

Salt and black pepper

1 cup all-purpose flour

1 large white onion, diced

8 ounces white button or cremini mushrooms, stemmed and chopped

4 garlic cloves, minced

1 (32-ounce) carton beef broth

1 (15-ounce) can hominy

1 (15-ounce) can kidney beans

1 (15-ounce) can pinto beans

2 (4-ounce) cans diced green chiles

2 (10-ounce) cans diced tomatoes and green chiles

2 (15-ounce) cans stewed tomatoes

2 tablespoons Worcestershire sauce

4 russet potatoes, cut into bite-size pieces

4 large carrots, sliced ½ inch thick

2 bay leaves

1. In a large cast-iron skillet over medium-high heat, cook the bacon for 4 to 5 minutes, until about three-quarters done. Transfer to a large pot. Reserve the bacon grease in the skillet.

2. Place the meat in a large bowl and season well with salt and pepper. Sprinkle in ½ cup of the flour and toss to coat.

3. Add half of the meat to the same skillet the bacon was cooked in. Cook over medium heat until the outside of the meat has browned. Transfer to the pot with the bacon. Repeat with the remaining meat.

4. Add the onion to the skillet and cook for about 4 minutes, stirring occasionally.

5. Stir in the mushrooms and cook, stirring occasionally, until they are soft, about 4 minutes. Stir in the garlic and continue to cook for another 2 minutes, giving it a stir or two. Sprinkle in the remaining ½ cup flour and mix well. Add the contents to the pot.

6. Stir in the broth, hominy, kidney beans, pinto beans, green chiles, diced tomatoes and green chiles, stewed tomatoes, Worcestershire sauce, potatoes, carrots, and bay leaves. Cover and cook over medium heat for 45 minutes. Reduce the heat to low and simmer for another 45 minutes. Remove the bay leaves and serve warm.

One of my favorite soups is a good ol' fashioned 'mater soup. I think we've outdone that canned stuff with a homemade version mixed with parsley, basil, a little cayenne, and, of course, cream. Save time here by using crushed canned tomatoes and sautéing them up with onions. Feel free to adjust the seasonings to your taste: Herbs such as thyme or rosemary can also be added. Of course, it's the perfect pairing with a grilled cheese sandwich.

CREAMY TOMATO SOUP

MAKES ABOUT 10 SERVINGS

PREP TIME: 10 MINUTES

TOTAL TIME: 40 MINUTES

2 tablespoons unsalted butter

1 tablespoon olive oil or avocado oil

2 yellow onions, chopped

5 (15-ounce) cans crushed tomatoes

½ to ¾ cup chopped fresh parsley

¼ to ½ cup chopped fresh basil or 2 tablespoons dried

2½ cups heavy cream

1 tablespoon garlic powder

¼ to ½ teaspoon cayenne pepper

1. In a large skillet over medium heat, melt the butter with the oil. Add the onions and cook, stirring occasionally, until the onions are tender, about 5 minutes.

2. Place the onions in a blender and add 2 cans of the tomatoes, the parsley, and basil. Blend until smooth.

3. Pour the contents into a large pot over medium heat. Stir in the cream, garlic powder, and cayenne pepper.

4. Place the remaining 3 cans tomatoes in the blender and blend until smooth. Stir into the pot.

5. Bring to a boil, then reduce the heat to a simmer and cook for 30 minutes, stirring occasionally. Serve warm.

"In times of hardship, just remember, this ain't no step for a stepper."

CODES OF THE COWBOY, CHUCK WAGON ETIQUETTE, AND COWBOY LORE

CODES

Never cut in front of another man horseback.

Remove your hat before eating at the table.

Take care of your livestock and family before yourself.

Be humble and respectful of others.

Never judge a man by the horse he rides or the hat on his head.

Leave a gate, open or closed, like you found it.

Honor God, family, and country.

Never ride another man's horse without first asking permission.

Don't tell others what you can do—show them.

CHUCK WAGON ETIQUETTE

Don't spit in camp.

Always ask permission from the cook before coming into camp.

Don't ride your horse or drive your truck close to camp, to prevent dusting the cook.

Don't talk politics or religion under the fly of the wagon.

Don't pitch a teepee close to the wagon.

It's rude to ask the cook what's for supper.

Never take the last helping of food.

No swearing in camp if women or children are present.

Cowboy Lore

If you compete with change in your pocket, it might be all you win.

Horseshoes can bring good luck. Hang a horseshoe heel up, so that the shoe collects good luck. If the heels point down, your good luck will run out.

A saddle bronc rider always puts the right foot in the stirrup first.

Cut off the head of a snake and bury it. Cut off the rattles and keep them for luck. Turn the snake belly side up for rain.

A horse with swirls under its mane on the neck indicates a good horse.

A dog with spots on the roof of its mouth will be a good dog.

THE *REAL FEEL* OF FIRE
GRILLING AND SMOKING

Fire and smoke have been something folks have been drawn to for centuries. There is just something mesmerizing, frightening, and intriguing about the two. If you fire up the grill in the backyard, the initial aroma of smoke gives your taste buds the anticipation of meat or lightly charred vegetables. But remember when I said you just want to get closer to it? Well, that also depends on the weather. I've cooked in every condition Mother Nature can throw at you. Besides the wind, heat is the worst to cook in with a fire, whether it's grilling or Dutch-oven cooking.

I got a call one time to cook for two hundred folks in southern Georgia in July. I was about to say, "Are y'all crazy?!" but the feller on the phone told me it was a benefit to buy car seats and strollers for the Safe and Sober Foundation. Well, how could I say no to that? I took the job.

I loaded the chuck wagon on the flatbed trailer; the stove was nestled behind the wagon. I packed six 16-inch Dutch ovens, five 12-inch Dutch ovens, and a steam table (for keeping the food warm) I had constructed out of galvanized tin that ran off a propane tank. I was loaded to the brim when I took off for the twelve-hundred-mile trip.

I'm sure y'all have heard of a little thing they call the heat index. It's when temperature and humidity are factored together to give what they call the "real feel" temperature. So, when you take a temperature of 96°F plus 80 percent humidity, it is just miserable, and I don't need a heat index to tell me that . . . I need a windchill. But it was me

that was hired for this sweat lodge event, so it was me that would get it done.

I got all my equipment unloaded and set up camp. The meat was seasoned and resting in the YETI ice chest in the shade. I was pretty much the only one around because even the locals didn't want to stay in camp for very long. I could hear them say, "This feller is either really tough or really crazy for cooking by the fire in this weather." They were all like a bunch of black cows on a hot day—they shaded up and watched from a cooler distance.

However, when the first steak went on the grill, I knew what would happen. It's the magic of smoke and a little breeze that drifted in their direction. It began with just one brave soul who meandered over, like one of them ol' lot shy cows. He stood about forty yards from camp, sniffing the breeze like a Beagle hunting bacon. That's when I knew I had them. To entice the rest of these early visitors, I added some mesquite chunks and let the smoke roll. *Real feel* or not, they *really* wanted some of that goodness my wood stove was grilling up. With each filet I slung on the grill, more and more sniffers showed up. Ten red and sweating onlookers quickly turned into forty, then eighty, like moths to a lantern. I heard one of them say as he wiped the sweat from his brow, "That smoke is so hypnotizing. I was just fine in the shade, and the next thing you know, I am here, melting in this heat, hoping that he might drop a bite in the grass."

"This might be the hottest day I have ever cooked over a fire in, and I'm so glad that y'all came to visit," I told them.

"Oh, we ain't here to visit," one answered. "We are just here for samples!"

As I took the second batch of steaks off the grill and placed them in the warming tray, I thought, *Do I need to put a padlock on them to keep them safe from this band of smoked and sweaty onlookers?* Soon the last of the steaks were on

the grill, and I added a little more wood just to entice them one last time. I was sure glad when the last ones were off the fire and I was away from the inferno. As I sat in the shade of the wagon, a young man came up to me and said, "Sir, I don't know what you done to get them fellers out from under that shade tree. All they have ever done at this event was complain about how hot it was and why didn't we move this gathering to winter."

I grinned and said, "It's the magic of smoke and fire. But I do agree with them that this would have been better in January during a snowstorm."

Now, it's time for y'all to gather up the wood, fire up the grill, and set out extra plates, 'cause there is no telling who may show up. But that is what cooking and sharing food is all about. Whether it's January or July, food just tastes better outside when enjoyed with the aroma of smoke and the *real feel* of sharing it with friends and family.

TOP TIPS FOR GRILLING

FUEL

You'll see us use the terms *indirect* and *direct heat* a lot in this chapter. To achieve this technique, rake all the coals to one side of the grill or smoker. The side of the grill that doesn't have any heat directly under it is the indirect heat side. The direct heat side has coals directly under the grates. This helps with better temperature control. The indirect heat side allows for a lower and slower cook time and more smoke penetration. The direct heat side is great for searing or adding quick heat to your meat and veggies.

I always recommend using hardwood in place of briquettes because of the better heat and flavor real wood provides. Hardwood lump charcoal is a great alternative to wood and offers the same benefits, just in charcoal form.

Be sure the coals are ashy white before grilling or smoking.

FLAVOR

To enhance the smoke flavor when cooking, soak wood chips in water for about 30 minutes. Add the chips on top of ashy white coals and replenish as needed, depending on the cook time.

Feel free to experiment with different types of woods and how they flavor food. In the majority of our recipes, I start with oak for a base. I will sometimes add mesquite to that for a heartier smoke flavor. I like to pair fruitwood with pork and chicken. For beef, I tend to use more mesquite and oakwoods. Hickory is a popular smoking wood but can be overpowering with too much smoke. Alderwood provides a nice, mellow smoke flavor and pairs well with fish.

Don't be afraid to combine different woods while cooking. All hardwoods make a different smoke and a different heat, and combining flavors can really enhance the taste of your food.

GRATE CARE

Be sure the grill grates are cleaned before you begin. The easiest way to clean grates is using a wire brush when the grates are hot. It's best if you clean the grates immediately after use because left-on food and ingredients can break down the grates.

Oil the grates after cleaning to keep them in good shape. Pour a little food grade oil on a clean, lint-free rag and rub over warm grates. It doesn't take much oil, and this is particularly important to do on cast-iron and stainless-steel grates.

Always oil or grease the grates before cooking. Butter spray can be dangerous as it will flame up when sprayed. You can simply use an oiled rag over the grates. When cooking fish, be sure to generously oil, as fish tends to stick more than other foods.

When storing your grill for a long period of time, remove the grates and place in a paper sack, which will help keep out moisture.

If y'all can't decide if you should throw a burger or a hot dog on the grill, we have solved the problem! This is an easy recipe to accomplish, and your backyard BBQ will become the talk of the town. Seasoned ground beef is rolled out thinly with whole green chiles and wrapped around a grilled hot dog. We then throw it on the fire for a double meat–double grilled hot dog and hamburger combo. Be sure to use a hoagie bun, because a regular hot dog bun won't be big enough to hold all this grilled goodness.

ALL-AMERICAN BURGER DOG

MAKES 4 SERVINGS

PREP TIME: 15 MINUTES
TOTAL TIME: 25 MINUTES

4 bun-length all-beef hot dogs
2 pounds 80% lean ground beef

Salt and black pepper
4 green chiles, roasted and peeled, or 1 (4-ounce) can whole green chiles

4 hoagie buns
Softened butter, for spreading
1 to 2 cups shredded cheddar cheese

1. Clean, oil, and preheat the grill to between 400°F and 450°F. Grill the hot dogs until slightly charred. Set aside in a warm place.

2. Separate the ground beef into 4 equal patties. Place 1 patty in between plastic wrap and roll or pat out into a circle about ⅛ inch thick. It should be big enough to wrap around a hot dog. Repeat with the remaining patties. Season the top of the patties with salt and pepper.

3. Place a green chile in the middle of each patty and place a hot dog on top. Using the plastic wrap, roll the hamburger meat around the hot dog. Pinch the ends to seal.

4. Reduce the grill temperature to between 375°F and 400°F and grill until evenly browned and the juices run clear, about 5 minutes. Be sure not to mash the dog while grilling, which will release the juices.

5. Meanwhile, lightly butter the inside of the hoagie rolls and toast over the grill. Flip over and top with cheese. Keep on the grill until the cheese has slightly melted. Top with the burger dogs and serve immediately topped with your favorite condiments.

Brisket is a staple cut of beef here in our neck of the woods, and it sure has been made popular in the BBQ world. Smoking a brisket is the best way to cook it because it's done over a low heat for a longer time to create a tender piece of beef. After smoking awhile, cut the cap off, which is going to make the burnt ends. These are slathered in a honey, garlic, and brown sugar glaze to create a good caramelization. Be sure to cut this against the grain for maximum tenderness. You can also have your butcher trim the brisket before smoking. If you have any left over, use it in our Texas Twinkies (page 51).

SMOKED BRISKET WITH BURNT ENDS

MAKES 6 TO 8 SERVINGS

PREP TIME: 6 HOURS AND 30 MINUTES

TOTAL TIME: 11 HOURS AND 45 MINUTES

Juice of 2 limes

1 (9- to 10-pound) whole brisket, trimmed

Salt and black pepper

Apple or cherry juice, for spraying

¼ cup Worcestershire sauce

2 tablespoons honey

2 tablespoons light brown sugar

1 teaspoon garlic powder

1. Rub the lime juice on all sides of the brisket. Generously rub salt and pepper all around to evenly coat. Cover and place in the fridge for at least 6 hours or up to overnight. Remove the brisket from the fridge about 30 minutes before cooking to bring to room temperature.

2. Clean, oil, and preheat the smoker to 225°F. I like to use a blend of oakwood and mesquite. Place the brisket on the smoker, fat side up, and smoke for 1 hour. Flip the brisket over and smoke for 1½ hours.

3. Remove the brisket from the smoker and generously spray with the fruit juice. Wrap the brisket in foil and seal. Return to the smoker and cook for 3 hours.

4. In a small bowl, mix together the Worcestershire sauce, honey, brown sugar, and garlic powder.

5. Remove the foil from the brisket and cut off the cap. Keep the brisket flat wrapped until ready to serve. Cut the cap into bite-size pieces, toss into the Worcestershire sauce mixture, and coat well.

6. Place the cap pieces on the hot smoker and cook, rotating occasionally, until the sauce caramelizes and chars, 10 to 15 minutes. For a smokier flavor, close the lid while cooking.

Sometimes I have to jazz up my veggies to eat them, and this is a great way to get some mushrooms in your diet. Soak the mushrooms in beef broth before stuffing to give them a richer flavor and grill them up faster. We're stuffing them with a good helping of cream cheese, sautéed bell pepper, garlic, green chiles, and sausage. I like to top them with panko bread crumbs to give them some crunch.

CREAM CHEESE, SAUSAGE, AND PEPPER–STUFFED MUSHROOMS

MAKES ABOUT 6 SERVINGS

PREP TIME: 20 MINUTES

TOTAL TIME: 30 MINUTES

½ pound ground breakfast sausage

4 tablespoons butter

½ red bell pepper, diced

½ yellow onion, diced

1 Anaheim or green chile, roasted and diced

2 garlic cloves, minced

15 white button mushrooms

2 cups beef broth

¼ to ⅓ cup Panko bread crumbs

4 ounces cream cheese, softened

½ to 1 cup shredded Parmesan cheese

1. In a medium cast-iron skillet over medium-high heat, brown the sausage, stirring occasionally, about 5 minutes. Drain and discard the grease. Transfer the sausage to a small bowl, cover, and set aside.

2. In the same skillet, melt the butter over medium heat. Stir in the bell pepper, onion, Anaheim chile, and garlic. Cook, stirring occasionally, until the flavors release and the vegetables soften slightly, about 5 minutes. Set aside.

3. Remove the stems from the mushrooms and carefully spoon out the inside gills. Place in a shallow pan and pour the broth around and in the mushrooms, enough to nearly cover. Let soak no more than 5 minutes, then drain.

4. In a small cast-iron skillet, toast the bread crumbs over medium heat until lightly browned and crisp.

5. Stuff each mushroom with 1 to 1½ teaspoons of cream cheese, followed by about 1½ teaspoons of the vegetable mix, then 1½ teaspoons of sausage. Top with bread crumbs.

6. Clean, oil, and preheat the grill to between 275°F and 300°F. Place the mushrooms on the grill and close the lid. Cook for 5 to 8 minutes, or until the mushrooms begin to soften.

7. Sprinkle each mushroom with 1 to 2 teaspoons of Parmesan cheese. Close the lid and cook just until the cheese melts. Serve warm.

Smoked bologna, also known as red rind steak, is a masterpiece of culinary art. If you grew up like me, fried bologna sandwiches were a delicacy. This recipe may even replace the holiday ham! Bologna is rubbed generously in a brown sugar and Dijon mustard glaze then topped with a little grated jalapeño. As it smokes, the flavor penetrates into the skin, and the sauce creates a great caramelization all around the outside.

SMOKED BOLOGNA

MAKES 10 TO 12 SERVINGS

PREP TIME: 10 MINUTES

TOTAL TIME: 3 HOURS AND 50 MINUTES

5 pounds beef bologna

½ cup packed light brown sugar

1 tablespoon onion powder

¼ cup honey Dijon mustard

1 tablespoon Worcestershire sauce

1 tablespoon coarsely ground black pepper

6 garlic cloves

About 1 cup lemon-lime soda

1 jalapeño, grated

1. Clean, oil, and preheat the grill or smoker to 250°F.

2. Take the bologna out of the fridge about 30 minutes before smoking to bring to room temperature.

3. In a small bowl, mix together the brown sugar, onion powder, Dijon mustard, Worcestershire sauce, and pepper.

4. Remove the packaging and rind from the bologna. Cut a V shape out of the top, long side of the bologna, about 1 inch deep.

5. Along both sides of the bologna, cut a diamond pattern about ¼ to ½ inch deep. This will allow more seasoning and smoke to penetrate.

6. Poke six holes throughout the sides of the bologna and press the garlic cloves deep inside.

7. Place the bologna in a large cast-iron skillet and pour the soda in the bottom of the skillet to generously cover (you may need a little more or less soda depending on your skillet).

8. Sprinkle the jalapeño into the V-shaped notch. Spread the brown sugar mixture generously all over the bologna with a spatula or spoon. Poke a knife down the middle of the notch in several places to allow the seasonings to penetrate more.

9. Cook for about 3 hours, or until a good crust develops on the bologna and the diamond pattern opens up slightly. Add a few more pieces of wood every 30 to 45 minutes to keep the temperature constant and to enhance the smoke flavor. I prefer to add apple or other fruitwood.

10. Remove from the heat and let cool about 10 minutes before slicing.

Are y'all ready to take your burger experience to the highest level? With this smoked bacon brisket burger, your taste buds will just hop up and dance a jig right there in your mouth with every bite. Using ground brisket instead of the traditional ground beef will give this burger a richer, beefy flavor.

BRISKET BURGER WITH SMOKED BACON

MAKES 4 SERVINGS

PREP TIME: 30 MINUTES

TOTAL TIME: 40 MINUTES

1 (2-pound) untrimmed ground brisket flat

8 slices thick-cut bacon

½ tablespoon salt

½ tablespoon garlic powder

½ tablespoon smoked paprika

½ tablespoon coarsely ground black pepper

4 slices cheddar cheese

Softened butter, for spreading

4 hamburger buns

4 slices pepper jack cheese

Sliced tomato, for topping (optional)

Sliced onion, for topping (optional)

Lettuce, for topping (optional)

Burger Sauce (recipe follows)

1. Divide the brisket into 4 equal parts and pat into ½-inch-thick patties. Cover with plastic and place in the fridge for at least 30 minutes before grilling. This will help the patties stay together.

2. Clean, oil, and preheat the grill to between 400°F and 450°F. Move the coals to one side of the grill for indirect and direct heat. Place the bacon on the indirect heat side of the grill, close the lid, and cook until crispy, about 4 minutes each side. Set aside and keep warm.

3. In a small bowl, combine the salt, garlic powder, paprika, and pepper. Sprinkle the seasoning on both sides of the patties and pat in right before grilling.

4. Oil the grill and place the patties on the direct heat side of the grill. Cook for about 4 minutes on each side, or until the internal temperature reaches 160°F. Right before the burgers are done, top with a slice of cheddar cheese to melt slightly.

5. Meanwhile, butter the inside of the buns and place on the grill to toast. Right before removing, add a slice of pepper jack cheese to the bottom bun until slightly melted.

6. Remove the burgers and the buns from the grill. Add any desired toppings, then generously drizzle with the burger sauce and serve immediately.

BURGER SAUCE

MAKES ABOUT 1 CUP

PREP TIME: 5 MINUTES

TOTAL TIME: 35 MINUTES

½ cup mayonnaise

¼ cup ketchup

¼ cup mustard

2 tablespoons honey

1 tablespoon Worcestershire sauce

2 teaspoons hot sauce

2 teaspoons minced garlic

In a small bowl, combine all the ingredients. Cover and place in the fridge for at least 30 minutes before serving.

Also known as drunken chicken, this method of smoking a yard bird will make you wonder why you haven't done this all the time. The key is to insert a half-full beer can infused with rosemary, thyme, and garlic into the cavity of the chicken. As it cooks, the steam will leave the chicken very tender. We have also made a wild plum sauce glaze to add a little sweetness to this bird.

WILD PLUM–GLAZED BEER CAN CHICKEN

MAKES ABOUT 6 SERVINGS

PREP TIME: 1 HOUR AND 5 MINUTES

TOTAL TIME: 2 HOURS AND 20 MINUTES

1 tablespoon smoked paprika

1 tablespoon dry mustard

1 tablespoon garlic powder

2 teaspoons salt

½ tablespoon ancho chile powder

½ tablespoon chili powder

½ tablespoon coarsely ground black pepper

1 (4- to 5-pound) whole chicken

Olive oil

1 (12-ounce) can beer, at room temperature

3 sprigs fresh rosemary or 1 tablespoon dried

½ tablespoon dried thyme

2 garlic cloves, minced

⅓ cup chipotle chiles in adobo sauce

½ cup pitted wild plums, or ¾ cup plum jelly

1 tablespoon Worcestershire sauce

⅓ cup packed light brown sugar

4 whole cloves

1 stick butter, melted

1. In a small bowl, combine the paprika, dry mustard, garlic powder, salt, ancho chile powder, chili powder, and pepper.

2. Remove any of the innards from the chicken and pat dry with paper towels. Generously rub the chicken with olive oil. Place the bird on a sheet pan and generously season the chicken with the seasoning mixture.

3. With a can opener, remove the top portion of the beer can and pour half of the beer out. Add the rosemary, thyme, and garlic to the beer can.

4. Arrange the chicken over the beer can so the chicken is standing upright with the beer can in its cavity. Place the bird in the fridge for at least 1 hour.

5. Meanwhile, place the chipotle chiles, wild plums, Worcestershire sauce, brown sugar, and cloves in a blender and blend well. Transfer to a medium bowl, cover, and place in the fridge until ready to use.

6. Clean, oil, and preheat the grill to 350°F. I prefer to use a blend of mesquite, oakwood, and applewood. Move the coals to one side of the grill for indirect and direct heat. Place the chicken on the indirect heat side of the grill, close the lid, and cook for 1 hour.

7. After 1 hour, begin generously basting the chicken with the butter every 15 minutes for an additional 1 hour, or until the internal temperature of the chicken is 150°F.

Recipe continues ➤

8. Generously brush the plum sauce on the chicken and continue cooking until the internal temperature of the chicken reaches 165°F. Brush a couple more times with the plum sauce, then remove the can from the chicken and tent the chicken with foil. Let rest for about 10 minutes before serving.

"If you climb in the saddle, you better be ready for the ride."

To me, a chicken thigh, with its combination of light and dark meat, has the most flavor of any piece on the bird. We start out by boiling this chicken to reduce the cooking time on the grill. This also makes the bones easier to remove. Stuff these thighs with cream cheese, garlic, and a seasoning mixture of onion powder, mustard, and brown sugar. Don't forget to glaze often with the whiskey honey glaze to boost the flavor.

DRUNKEN STUFFED CHICKEN THIGHS

MAKES 6 SERVINGS

PREP TIME: 20 MINUTES

TOTAL TIME: 50 MINUTES

3 tablespoons whiskey or bourbon

2 tablespoons honey

2 jalapeños, diced

6 bone-in chicken thighs

4 ounces cream cheese, softened

4 garlic cloves, minced

2 teaspoons onion powder

1 teaspoon dry mustard

3 tablespoons light brown sugar

6 slices thick-cut bacon

1. Clean, oil, and preheat the grill or smoker to between 350°F and 375°F. Move the coals to one side of the grill for indirect and direct heat.

2. In a small bowl, whisk together the whiskey, honey, and jalapeños.

3. In a large saucepan, place the chicken thighs and cover with water. Bring to a boil for 15 minutes. Strain the thighs from the water and let cool.

4. In a small bowl, whisk together the cream cheese, garlic, onion powder, dry mustard, and brown sugar.

5. Carefully cut around the bone of the thighs to remove and discard. Lay the thighs out on a cutting board, skin side down. Spoon 1 to 2 tablespoons of the cream cheese mixture down the middle of each thigh where the bone was removed. Fold the thigh over and wrap the skin around. Wrap a piece of bacon around the thigh, covering the open sides, and secure with one or two toothpicks.

6. Place the thighs on the indirect heat side of the grill. Grill for about 10 minutes on each side.

7. Generously baste the thighs with the whiskey glaze. Let cook for 3 minutes, flip the thighs over, and baste the opposite side. Cook for another 3 minutes, or until the internal temperature reaches 165°F.

8. Remove and baste again before serving. Serve warm.

This has been a holiday tradition at our home. Smoking the ham brings out so much more flavor than just baking it in the oven. This is twice smoked because we're starting out with an already-smoked ham and smoking it again with a rich Coca-Cola, honey, and clove glaze for a great holiday flavor. At the end of smoking, we are breaking out the big torch to give this a great caramelization. Don't worry if you don't have a torch because this can be done under the broiler also.

TWICE-SMOKED BOURBON HAM

MAKES ABOUT 20 SERVINGS

PREP TIME: 5 MINUTES

TOTAL TIME: 6 HOURS AND 30 MINUTES

1 (15-pound) bone-in smoked and cured ham

¾ cup packed light brown sugar

2 teaspoons onion powder

1 teaspoon ground cinnamon

2 teaspoons chili powder

2 teaspoons smoked paprika

¼ cup whiskey

½ (12-ounce) can Coca-Cola

⅓ cup honey

¼ cup packed light brown sugar

2 teaspoons ground cloves

½ stick unsalted butter

1. Clean, oil, and preheat the smoker to 250°F.

2. Take the ham out of the fridge about 1 hour before cooking to bring to room temperature.

3. In a small bowl, combine the brown sugar, onion powder, cinnamon, chili powder, and paprika.

4. Generously rub the ham with the seasoning mixture. Place the ham on the smoker and add a few chunks of cherry- or applewood. Close the lid and cook for 15 to 20 minutes per pound, or until the internal temp is 130°F.

5. Meanwhile, add the whiskey and Coca-Cola to a saucepan over medium-low heat and bring to a simmer. Stir in the honey, brown sugar, cloves, and butter. Bring to a low boil, then reduce the heat and simmer for about 2 minutes.

6. Remove the ham from the smoker and place on a cookie sheet. Take a knife and score the top of the ham ½ inch deep in a diamond pattern.

7. Place the ham back on the smoker and brush about a quarter of the glaze over the ham. Cook for an additional 15 minutes, basting about every 5 minutes.

8. Use a culinary torch or propane torch to caramelize the top until the glaze begins to brown. If you don't have a torch, you can transfer the ham to a conventional oven and broil on high for about 5 minutes, or until the top has caramelized.

9. Remove the ham from the smoker and transfer to a large baking dish. Cover with foil and let rest for about 10 minutes. Slice the ham against the grain and serve warm.

Let's change catfish up a bit. Instead of traditionally frying these fillets, we'll smoke them for a richer and deeper flavor that only the grill can provide. These whisker fish, as I call them, are going to rest in a seasoning mixture of honey, vinegar, chili powder, and herbs. I like to use alderwood because it gives a mellow smoke that blends well with fish of any kind. Fruitwood also works well.

SMOKY CATFISH WITH HOMEMADE TARTAR SAUCE

MAKES 4 SERVINGS

PREP TIME: 10 MINUTES

TOTAL TIME: 1 HOUR AND 10 MINUTES

½ cup mayonnaise

2 to 3 tablespoons diced dill pickle

1 tablespoon fresh lemon juice

2 tablespoons capers, drained and diced

3 teaspoons Worcestershire sauce

2 teaspoons prepared horseradish

½ cup olive oil

3 tablespoons honey

½ tablespoon red wine vinegar

2 teaspoons dill seed

2 teaspoons chili powder

3 teaspoons smoked paprika

2 teaspoons dried parsley

2 teaspoons crushed dried rosemary

4 catfish fillets, rinsed and patted dry

1. Add about 2 heaping handfuls of alderwood chunks (or wood of your choice) to water to soak for about 10 minutes.

2. Meanwhile, in a small bowl, combine the mayonnaise, dill pickle, lemon juice, capers, Worcestershire sauce, and horseradish. Cover and place in the fridge for at least 30 minutes before serving.

3. In a medium bowl, mix together the olive oil, honey, vinegar, dill seed, chili powder, paprika, parsley, and rosemary. Dredge the fillets through the mixture to coat well on both sides and place in a zipper-top plastic bag. Pour the remaining marinade in the bag and shake to coat the fillets again. Seal and place in the fridge for at least 4 hours.

4. Clean, oil, and preheat the grill to 225°F. Move the coals to one side of the grill for indirect and direct heat. Strain the alderwood from the water and add to the coals.

5. Place the catfish on the indirect heat side of the grill. Close the lid and let cook for 45 minutes to 1 hour, or until the fish is white and flaky. About 20 minutes into cooking, add more wood chips to create more smoke.

6. Remove the fillets from the heat and let cool slightly before serving with the tartar sauce.

This is probably Shannon's favorite thing to order at a Mexican restaurant. We are starting out with freshwater fillets marinated in a chili powder, smoked paprika, and lime bath that are then char-grilled. To enhance that rich, smoky flavor, top these with our cool and creamy coleslaw that has just a touch of liquid smoke. You can serve these up on a store-bought tortilla, but if you want more flavor, be sure to try these with our Easy Corn Tortillas (page 105).

GRILLED WHITE FISH TACOS
WITH SMOKY COLESLAW

MAKES 4 SERVINGS

PREP TIME: 1 HOUR
TOTAL TIME: 1 HOUR AND 15 MINUTES

Juice of 1 lime
2 tablespoons olive oil
1 clove garlic, minced

1½ teaspoons chili powder
1 teaspoon ground cumin
½ teaspoon smoked paprika
4 (4-ounce) freshwater white fish fillets, such as perch, catfish, or walleye

4 store-bought corn tortillas or Easy Corn Tortillas (page 105)
Smoky Coleslaw (recipe follows)
Queso fresco, for topping (optional)
Sliced avocado, for topping (optional)

1. In a small bowl, mix together the lime juice, olive oil, garlic, chili powder, cumin, and paprika.

2. Cut the fish into large strips and place in a zipper-top plastic bag. Add the seasoning mixture, seal the bag, and toss to coat the fish. Place in the fridge for 1 hour.

3. Clean, oil, and preheat the grill to between 400°F and 450°F. Grill the fillets about 3 to 4 minutes per side, depending on the thickness of fish. Before turning the fish, be sure the underside is white and firmed up slightly. The fish is done when it is white and flaky.

4. Remove from the grill and let rest for 2 to 3 minutes. Crumble the fish into the tortillas and top with the slaw and, if desired, the queso fresco and avocado. Serve immediately.

SMOKY COLESLAW

MAKES ABOUT ½ CUP

PREP TIME: 5 MINUTES

TOTAL TIME: 1 HOUR AND 5 MINUTES

4 tablespoons sour cream

2 tablespoons mayonnaise

2 teaspoons prepared horseradish

2 teaspoons lemon juice

½ teaspoon liquid smoke

1 tablespoon dried dill

1 teaspoon chopped dried ancho chile

1 teaspoon sugar

1 (16-ounce) bag tricolor coleslaw

1. In a small bowl, mix together the sour cream, mayonnaise, horseradish, lemon juice, liquid smoke, dill, chopped chile, and sugar until smooth.

2. Place the coleslaw in a medium bowl and stir in the dressing mixture. Cover and place in the fridge at least 1 hour. Stir before serving.

THE DAY SPOTTY WENT TO TOWN

Some years back, a feller asked me to go rope Spotty, a horned cow of his that was nuttier than a five-pound fruitcake. She'd gotten some barbed wire wrapped around her foot, and he needed me to remove it. I loaded up Red, my trusty red sorrel horse, and drove across the Red River. I found the old cow hiding in a plum thicket, with a bracelet of barbed wire wrapped tightly on her back leg.

I built a loop and rode to her quickly like the Pony Express. She didn't act scared at all—in fact, she was rather bold and came barreling at me just as I roped her. That's when things got a little "Western," as they say. She gave Red a hard horn to the flank, and when he began to pitch, she drove a horn right in his derriere—a little disrespectful, I thought! Well, I like a challenge, but I do prefer an even fight!

That barbed wire was dragging off her about ten feet in length and had captured remnants of old feed sacks, prickly pear, and branches. Red just doesn't like barbed wire and hooking bovines at the same time. When I finally got her pinned down, I cut that barbed wire off her, but the cut around her hock was deep. I made a corporate decision to take her by the vet clinic and doctor her in their squeeze chute before returning the lovely lady to the pasture.

Dad used to work at the vet clinic for years, and the doctor never minded when I borrowed the chute. However, to my surprise, the regular doctor was on vacation that day, and a young lady was his temporary replacement. She was fresh out of veterinary school and itching for some action. I don't mean this disrespectful, but I think she had specialized in small animals, like guinea pigs and teacup poodles, and Spotty didn't resemble anything small.

When I arrived at the clinic and explained the situation, she was having no part in me just running her chute. She wanted to do everything by the book and perform a full examination on the cow. I explained to her that Spotty didn't like no doctorin' and sure didn't take a liking to any exam. But after a dictionary full of big veterinarian words, I gave in.

I ran Spotty down the chute, tied a leg up, and waited for the vet to scrub in. You would have thought she was going to do open-heart surgery the way she was going over textbooks and laying out instruments. And the longer we waited, the more hostile Spotty became.

The vet washed out the wound with iodine, packed it with salve, and wrapped it up. I asked her to let the squeeze off Spotty's head so I could back her down the chute and onto the trailer. "I can do it!" the young vet confidently answered. I'm no psychic, but I saw a wreck fixin' to happen.

About that time, a feller came out the door of the office, which emptied right into our working area. He was one of those clean fellers in a starched white shirt and brand-new boots. He looked like he hadn't ever gotten dirty a day in his life. I told him, "I wouldn't stand there; this goofy cow might get out and go the wrong way." In a somewhat cocky tone, he answered, "Now, don't you worry, son, I have been around wild cattle all of my life, and she don't bother me."

Since I was obviously surrounded by people smarter than me, I gave up. The vet pulled a Moses and opened the head gate wide enough to part the Red Sea. As soon as Spotty saw the light of day, she was greeting that feller with those horns she was so proud of. But it just so happened that her aim was a little off, and she pinned him against the wall right between her horns.

He did commence to holler and cuss quite a bit. I've seen and been a part of many a hooking, and since there wasn't any blood or bones exposed, I thought this feller could use a little hooking. His eyes were as white as his clean starched shirt, and he just kept screaming, "Get this damn cow off of me!" There was snot and spit flying everywhere from Spotty, and the only reply I could think of was, "Say, mister, you got a little something there on your boots."

Spotty finally got tired and gave up, and nothing was broken except maybe that feller's pride. I got Spotty on the trailer, and I think everyone was glad to see us loaded up.

Before driving off, I hollered from my pickup window, "Ma'am, thanks for making me change my mind. I thought today was going to be a little boring, but that was a pretty good wreck and I didn't even get a scratch. And, sir, I want to thank you for showing me how to handle *wild* cattle with horns. It was an excellent lesson on how to get between them horns and not on them!"

"Thank you!" That is what your slow cooker will be saying after the day off. I've done many a roast in a slow cooker, but when you can throw one on the grill and let that good low smoke penetrate it, you can't beat the flavor. Start off by searing this seasoned roast over the flames before it goes in the smoker to lock in flavor and moisture. When it is time, remove and add some butter and thyme to the top and then wrap with unwaxed butcher paper and cook until tender. There are a lot of serving possibilities with this roast. You can slice it and serve or chop it and mix with BBQ sauce for a sandwich.

MELT-IN-YOUR-MOUTH CHUCK ROAST

MAKES 6 TO 8 SERVINGS

PREP TIME: 3 HOURS

TOTAL TIME: 6 HOURS AND 55 MINUTES

1 (2½- to 3-pound) chuck roast

Juice of 1 lime

2 tablespoons Worcestershire sauce

1 tablespoon seasoned salt

1½ tablespoons coarsely ground black pepper

½ tablespoon garlic powder

1 tablespoon smoked paprika

½ tablespoon dry mustard

½ tablespoon onion powder

2 tablespoons butter

4 sprigs fresh thyme

1. Generously rub all sides of the roast with the lime juice, then the Worcestershire sauce.

2. In a small bowl, combine the seasoned salt, pepper, garlic powder, paprika, dry mustard, and onion powder.

3. Coat the roast well with the seasoning mixture on all sides. Cover and place in the fridge for at least 2 hours. Take the roast from the fridge about 1 hour before cooking to bring to room temperature.

4. Clean, oil, and preheat the grill to between 375°F and 400°F. I prefer to use a mixture of oakwood and mesquite. Move the coals to one side of the grill for indirect and direct heat. Sear the roast over direct heat for 4 to 5 minutes on each side.

5. Add a few chunks of apple- or cherrywood to the coals. Place the roast over the indirect heat side of the grill, close the lid, and smoke for about 40 minutes.

6. Remove the roast from the grill and place on unwaxed butcher paper. Place the butter and thyme on top of the roast and wrap in the butcher paper. Wrap in an additional sheet of paper to help seal in the moisture.

7. Place the roast back on the indirect heat side and let cook for 2½ to 3 hours at 250° to 275°F, or until the internal temperature is 200° to 225°F.

8. Remove the roast from the grill and place in a large pan and unwrap the meat. Reserve any juices to spoon over when serving, if desired. Let cool slightly before cutting and serving.

TIP This recipe will cut well into slices. If you prefer a more tender, fall-apart roast, cook an additional 45 minutes to 1 hour, or until the internal temperature is around 250°F.

This old classic is going on the smoker, and, folks, this is going to be the best meat loaf ever. I think what makes this meat loaf so special is the blending of beef and pork together. Instead of using ketchup or tomato sauce for a topping, we are making a special sauce with honey, horseradish, and adobo sauce for a bold flavor that caramelizes as it cooks.

SMOKED MEAT LOAF

MAKES 6 TO 8 SERVINGS

PREP TIME: 30 MINUTES

TOTAL TIME: 3 HOURS AND 10 MINUTES

1 cup honey

3 tablespoons adobo sauce

½ tablespoon prepared horseradish

½ tablespoon Worcestershire sauce

1½ tablespoons smoked paprika

2 pounds 80% lean ground beef

1 pound ground breakfast sausage

1 yellow onion, chopped

1 red bell pepper, diced

2 serrano chiles, stemmed, seeded, and diced

4 garlic cloves, minced

1 tablespoon seasoned salt

1 tablespoon coarsely ground black pepper

½ tablespoon garlic powder

1 large egg, beaten

¾ cup heavy cream

1 sleeve Ritz crackers, crushed

1 to 2 poblano chiles

1. In a small bowl, whisk together the honey, adobo sauce, horseradish, Worcestershire sauce, and ½ tablespoon of the paprika. Set aside.

2. In a large bowl, use your hands to mix together the ground beef and sausage. Mix in the onion, bell pepper, serranos, garlic, seasoned salt, pepper, the remaining 1 tablespoon paprika, and the garlic powder until well incorporated.

3. Mix in the egg, cream, and crackers.

4. Cover a large baking pan with plastic wrap or waxed paper. Evenly form the meat on top into a loaf about 12 inches in length.

5. Brush a light coat of the sauce mixture onto the meat and then roll up tightly, pulling the paper away as you roll. Discard the paper. Transfer the meat loaf to a plate and place in the fridge for 20 minutes. Reserve the remaining sauce.

6. Clean, oil, and preheat the grill or smoker to 250° to 275°F. I prefer a blend of mesquite and oakwood. Move the coals to one side of the grill for indirect and direct heat.

7. Remove the meat from the fridge and place on a wire rack. Set the rack on a large cast-iron skillet or pan and place on the indirect heat side of the grill. Close the lid and add a few more chunks of wood. Smoke for 30 minutes.

8. Baste the meat loaf with the sauce and continue basting about every 30 minutes for 2 hours, or until the internal temperature is about 160°F.

Recipe continues ➤

9. About 45 minutes before the meat loaf is done, add the poblanos to the grill, turning to evenly blister. Transfer to a zipper-top plastic bag with a little water for a few minutes. The steam will help release the skin. Remove the skin and seeds and cut into thin strips. Lay the strips over the meat loaf and let finish cooking 15 to 20 minutes.

10. Remove the loaf from the smoker and pour the remaining sauce over top. Cover with foil and let rest for about 10 minutes to allow the internal temperature to climb slightly. Slice and serve warm.

The filet is the tenderest cut of beef that comes off the hoof. It also is a good portion size if you aren't wanting a big cut of beef. Be sure you get thick-cut peppered bacon for more flavor. Wrap these in whole green chiles, which complements the bacon.

BACON-WRAPPED GREEN CHILE FILET

MAKES 2 SERVINGS

PREP TIME: 5 MINUTES
TOTAL TIME: 20 MINUTES

2 (8-ounce) beef filets

2 green chiles, roasted, peeled, and seeded

2 thick-cut slices peppered bacon

Salt and black pepper

1. Remove the filets from the fridge about 30 minutes before grilling to bring to room temperature.

2. Clean, oil, and preheat the grill to 225°F. Move the coals to one side of the grill for indirect and direct heat. If you have an adjustable grill, lower the grate as much as possible.

3. Cut the chiles in half lengthwise. Wrap each filet, along the outside edge, with the chiles followed by a strip of the bacon. Secure with a toothpick(s). Season both sides of the filet with salt and pepper.

4. Place the filets on the indirect heat side of the grill, close the lid, and cook for about 4 minutes on each side.

5. Flip the filets over and move to the direct heat side of the grill. With the lid open, cook for about 3 minutes on each side, or until the internal temperature is 130° to 135°F for medium-rare.

6. Remove the filets from the grill and let rest a few minutes before cutting. Remove the toothpicks before serving.

I do love a pork chop, but part of the problem with them is they can dry out easily when cooking. With this recipe, you'll have no more dry chops! The salt is the magic ingredient here and works by science with reverse osmosis. The brine draws the moisture to the surface of the chop and then soaks back in. You can make these chops in a good cast-iron skillet, but I prefer to throw it on the grill for a good char and smoke flavor.

JUICY BRINED PORK CHOP

MAKES 4 SERVINGS

PREP TIME: 24 HOURS
TOTAL TIME: 25 HOURS

2½ tablespoons coarsely ground salt

½ tablespoon coarsely ground black pepper

2 teaspoons garlic powder

1 teaspoon ancho chile powder

1 teaspoon seasoned salt

4 (1½-inch-thick) center-cut pork chops

Barbecue sauce, for basting

1. In a small bowl, combine the coarse salt, pepper, garlic powder, ancho chile powder, and seasoned salt. Rub in the seasoning on both sides of the chops.

2. Place a wire rack on a baking pan. Place the chops on the wire rack and in the fridge, uncovered, for 12 hours. Turn the chops over and leave in the fridge an additional 12 hours.

3. Remove the chops from the fridge about 30 minutes before grilling to bring to room temperature. Make a cut through the edge of the rind on each chop to prevent it from curling up while grilling.

4. Clean, oil, and preheat the grill to between 400°F and 450°F. I prefer a mix of oak- and applewoods. Move the coals to one side of the grill for direct and indirect heat.

5. Place the chops on the indirect heat side of the grill. Cook for about 30 to 40 minutes, or until the internal temperature is about 140°F.

6. Move the chops over to the direct heat side of the grill. Grill for 3 to 4 minutes per side, or until the internal temperature is 160°F and grill marks appear.

7. Generously baste both sides of the chops with barbecue sauce and cook an additional 1 to 2 minutes per side.

8. Remove the chops from the grill and let rest for about 5 minutes. Serve warm.

Tri tip is a common cut of beef out in the western United States, and the popularity of this great cut of meat is spreading like wildfire throughout other regions of the country too. Although it is a leaner cut of beef, it offers a decent amount of fat for a good buttery flavor. Our rub of ground coffee and coriander will also give this cut a unique flavor boost. Smoke this up and serve as a sandwich with our zesty sauce blend of garlic, horseradish, and honey.

TRI TIP SANDWICH
WITH ZESTY SAUCE

MAKES 8 SERVINGS

PREP TIME: 6 HOURS

TOTAL TIME: 7 HOURS AND 20 MINUTES

Juice of 1 lime

1 (3½- to 4-pound) tri tip, trimmed

¼ cup coffee grounds

¼ cup packed light brown sugar

¼ cup coarsely ground black pepper

¼ cup ground coriander

2 tablespoons dry mustard

2 tablespoons ancho chile powder

2 tablespoons seasoned salt

1 tablespoon garlic powder

8 hamburger buns

Lettuce, for serving

Red onion, thinly sliced, for serving

Zesty Sauce (recipe follows)

1. Rub the lime juice all over the tri tip.

2. In a small bowl, combine the coffee grounds, brown sugar, pepper, coriander, dry mustard, ancho chile powder, seasoned salt, and garlic powder. Generously rub the seasoning all over the tri tip. Cover and place in the fridge for at least 6 hours or up to overnight.

3. Take the tri tip out of the fridge about 30 minutes before cooking to bring to room temperature.

4. Clean, oil, and preheat the grill to 225° to 250°F. Move the coals to one side of the grill for indirect and direct heat.

5. Place the tri tip on the indirect heat side of the grill. Close the lid and smoke for 30 to 40 minutes, or until the internal temperature reaches about 115°F.

6. Remove the tri tip from the grill and double wrap it in unwaxed butcher paper. Place it back on the indirect heat side of the grill and cook another 20 minutes, or until the internal temperature reaches about 120°F.

7. Remove the tri tip from the grill and let rest for about 20 minutes. The internal temperature will climb to about 125°F. Thinly slice against the grain.

8. Toast the hamburger buns and place 4 to 6 ounces of meat on top of each bun. Top with lettuce, red onion, and Zesty Sauce. Serve immediately.

TIP Let the tri tip cool to room temperature, then chill it for about 30 minutes for easier slicing.

ZESTY SAUCE

MAKES ABOUT 1 CUP

PREP TIME: 5 MINUTES

TOTAL TIME: 35 MINUTES

½ cup mayonnaise

⅓ cup Worcestershire sauce

6 tablespoons prepared horseradish

¼ cup minced garlic

¼ cup honey

¼ cup sour cream

2 to 4 tablespoons coarsely ground black pepper

In a small bowl, whisk together all the ingredients. Cover and place in the fridge for at least 30 minutes before serving.

BEFORE THE ASHES GROW COLD

I was cooking for a ranch in the late nineties near Abilene, Texas, during spring works. We were in for about three weeks, and I was using the ranch's wagon and team of horses, so let's just say it was like cooking in someone else's kitchen. I spent a lot of time looking through drawers for utensils, spices, and so on. It was also a whole new crew to feed and new faces in camp. However, there was one constant that I knew, and that was cooking by fire. It doesn't matter where I am or whom I'm cooking for, I always know fire. We all have those things that we tend to gravitate toward to make us feel comfortable when we feel a little out of place or find ourselves in new surroundings. It's like riding your best horse—you just know it, and the two of you trust each other.

The days started early, and by that I mean around 3 a.m. I'd start the fire, put the coffee on, and start making bread. There was an older feller who came over every morning just as the coffee got ready. He would say his good mornings and ask if it was coffee yet. And every morning I told him, "You're right on time. I just got it ready." He then would pull up a chair next to ol' Bertha, my wood stove, and slowly take in the morning brew. As each morning went by, I noticed that he would always sit on the smoky side of the fire. I thought this was a little strange 'cause I've been around enough smoke to last me a lifetime.

On the fourth morning, he settled in again on the smoky side of the fire, and I finally had to ask, "Mac, you like the smoke?" He raised his head and looked at me through the white ashy haze of mesquite smoke, and just for a second he looked like a gray ghost with a hat on his head.

"Yep, Cookie," he answered. "I've been around fire most of my life, from branding fires to cooking fires. I've watched as their ashes grew cold and the last bit of light and heat flickered away like a candle in the dark." He paused for a moment as if he were scanning a lifetime in his mind and then began again. "Fire is like life. We all start as a flicker and with a little stoking we grow into a pretty good flame. Now, as we continue to burn, we need a little kindling at times to keep us going. Someone's got to gather the wood and feed us from time to time. To be considered a fire worth building in the first place, we have duties that we must perform. Like light on the darkest of nights and heat to nourish those around us who are counting on us. As I see it, you can throw some ol' rotten sticks on that fire or you can feed it with what it needs and that is good hardwood, something that is going to last. It's like your word. If it doesn't last long or do what it's supposed to, it's like that rotten stick: It's gone pretty quick and has no value to sustaining the fire as it burns. You better stoke that fire every once in a while to keep it burning bright, just like we need a little push now and then to keep going."

As he spoke, I noticed he had picked up a stick and was poking at the coals. I wondered how many fires he had sat around, how many times he had gathered wood to stoke the fire, and how many hot irons he had drug out of a branding fire to make their mark on a yearling's hide.

He slowly straightened up, his back still slightly bent as his old creaking bones began to pop. He thanked me for the coffee and the fire. As he walked back to his teepee and into the darkness, the smoke seemed to gather around him like a blanket. He stopped, turned around, and said, "I hope to be back before the ashes grow cold, Cookie."

As he got out of sight, I noticed my fire had lost some of its glow, so I went to get more wood and get on with the morning chores before everyone arrived for breakfast. As I threw a chunk of wood on the fire, I looked in the direction of Mac's teepee. All I could see was darkness and the faint sound of his spur rowels jingling in a perfect cadence. I thought about what Mac had said, and it reminded me of all the fires I had built through the years, the wood I had split, the countless gallons of coffee I had made, and the heavens that I had filled with smoke. It seemed that maybe at times I had taken that old smoke for granted. I had cussed it when I had wet or sorry wood that just set and smoldered, never making a flame. But, the more I thought about it, fire and smoke have taught me a lot about perseverance, patience, and just taking the time to enjoy life's little blessings. I guess we all should be so lucky to be baptized with a little smoke and some wise words around an ol' fire.

How do you make a classic event better? Combine sausage and beef, then throw those meatballs on the smoker. But the meat may not be the star attraction here—it is the homemade sauce, thick, rich, and bubbling. Now toss in the smoked meatballs, and you're eating a cowboy Italian classic.

SPAGHETTI AND SMOKED MEATBALLS

MAKES ABOUT 6 SERVINGS

PREP TIME: 4 HOURS

TOTAL TIME: 4 HOURS AND 55 MINUTES

Meatballs

1 pound ground chuck

1 pound ground pork breakfast sausage

2 tablespoons Italian bread crumbs

2 tablespoons grated Parmesan cheese

1 tablespoon smoked paprika

1 tablespoon roasted fennel seeds

1 tablespoon garlic powder

½ tablespoon red pepper flakes

½ tablespoon Italian seasoning

½ tablespoon salt

½ tablespoon coarsely ground black pepper

½ tablespoon garlic powder

Sauce

10 Roma tomatoes

2 white onions

½ cup chopped fresh spinach

8 garlic cloves

1 (10-ounce) can diced tomatoes and green chiles, drained

3 tablespoons dried parsley

3 tablespoons dried basil

1 pound white button or cremini mushrooms, stemmed and chopped

½ cup dry red wine

2 tablespoons Worcestershire sauce

2 tablespoons Italian seasoning

1 teaspoon fennel seeds

Salt and black pepper

1 pound uncooked spaghetti

1. Make the meatballs: In a large bowl, combine the ground chuck and sausage. Add the remaining meatball seasonings and mix well with your hands. Cover and set in the fridge for at least 4 hours.

2. Make the sauce: Place the tomatoes in a large saucepan and cover with water. Cover and cook over medium-high heat until the skins crack, about 5 minutes.

3. Drain the tomatoes from the water and peel off the skins. Place the Roma tomatoes, onions, spinach, garlic cloves, diced tomatoes and green chiles, parsley, and basil in a blender and blend until smooth.

4. Pour the sauce into a large pot over medium-low heat. Stir in the mushrooms, wine, Worcestershire sauce, Italian seasoning, and fennel seeds. Season with salt and black pepper to taste. Cover and let simmer for about 25 minutes.

5. Meanwhile, clean, oil, and preheat the grill or smoker to 300°F. Move the coals to one side of the grill for direct and indirect heat.

6. Remove the meat from the fridge and form into 1½-inch balls.

7. Place the meatballs on the indirect heat side of the grill. Close the lid and smoke for about 20 minutes. Move the meatballs to the direct heat

side of the grill and cook for another 5 minutes, rotating as they cook.

8. Remove the meatballs from the grill and place them in the sauce. Simmer for about 30 minutes, stirring occasionally.

9. Meanwhile, cook the spaghetti according to package directions. Drain the pasta, top with meatballs and sauce, and serve immediately.

Just because a dish is good doesn't mean it has to be hard to make. We're rubbing this pork with mayonnaise, then coating it in seasoning to give it a good crust. Then it's basically set it and forget it. This is perfect to feed a crowd or save for leftovers, as the flavor intensifies as it sets. Top this with your favorite BBQ sauce, or for a thick and zesty flavor try our Red River Mud, available at KentRollins.com. If you have leftovers, use them in our Texas Twinkies (page 51).

APPLE-SMOKED PULLED PORK

MAKES 15 TO 20 SERVINGS, OR ABOUT 30 SANDWICHES

PREP TIME: 13 HOURS AND 30 MINUTES

TOTAL TIME: 20 HOURS AND 45 MINUTES

5 tablespoons smoked paprika

3 tablespoons seasoned salt

2 tablespoons coarsely ground black pepper

2 tablespoons chili powder

1 tablespoon onion powder

1 tablespoon dry mustard

½ tablespoon garlic powder

½ tablespoon ground cumin

1 (9- to 10-pound) pork butt or pork shoulder

½ cup mayonnaise

Apple juice, for spraying

½ (12-ounce) can lemon-lime soda

½ (12-ounce) can ginger ale

Sandwich rolls, for serving (optional)

Barbecue sauce, for serving (optional)

1. In a small bowl, combine the paprika, seasoned salt, pepper, chili powder, onion powder, dry mustard, garlic powder, and cumin.

2. Coat the pork lightly with the mayonnaise. Rub the seasoning mixture all over the pork. Place the pork in a large pan and cover. Place in the fridge for at least 12 hours.

3. Remove the pork from the fridge at least 1½ hours before cooking to bring to room temperature.

4. Meanwhile, clean, oil, and preheat the smoker or grill to 250°F. Add a few applewood chunks to the coals.

5. Place the pork in the smoker and cook for 3 to 4 hours, or until the internal temperature is 170°F. Every 30 to 45 minutes, generously spray the pork with the apple juice.

6. Remove the pork from the smoker and place in a large foil pan. Pour the lemon-lime and ginger ale sodas around the pork. Tightly seal up the pork with foil to seal in the moisture.

7. Return the pork to the smoker and cook for 2 to 3 hours, or until the temperature is 195° to 200°F.

8. Remove from the smoker and let the pork rest for 15 minutes. Shred and serve by itself or on sandwiches with barbecue sauce.

Okay, so I may not have seen many crabs crawling through any of our camps, but seafood is one of my favorite foods, and whenever I get the chance, I like to experiment with fish. When it comes to crab, most folks just boil them. But you know me and fire, so let's throw these fellers on the grill. The smoke penetrates the shells and gives them a lightly sweet and smoky flavor that is unique to crab legs and is sure easy to do.

SMOKED CRAB LEGS

MAKES 2 SERVINGS

PREP TIME: 5 MINUTES

TOTAL TIME: 30 MINUTES

2 sticks butter, melted

½ tablespoon ground coriander

2 teaspoons dried oregano

2 teaspoons smoked paprika

1 teaspoon garlic powder

1 teaspoon chopped fresh dill

1 teaspoon salt

1 teaspoon black pepper

2 pounds crab legs, thawed if frozen

Ice, for serving (optional)

1. Clean, oil, and preheat the grill or smoker to 200°F. I prefer a mix of apple- and alderwood. Move the coals to one side of the grill for indirect and direct heat.

2. In a small bowl, combine the butter, coriander, oregano, paprika, garlic powder, dill, salt, and pepper.

3. Place the crab legs on the indirect heat side of the grill and smoke for about 20 minutes. Generously baste the crab with the butter mixture about every 5 minutes while smoking.

4. Remove the crab from the grill. Serve warm or place over ice and serve chilled.

"Courage and strength will follow when you always lead with faith and heart."

OL' CHAMP AND THE
PICKING PALOOZA
DESSERTS

There is no better way to finish a meal than with a homemade dessert, fresh from the vine or the tree.

It had been a long Saturday morning of weekend chores doled out by Mama. My older brothers, Dale and Randy, were in charge of feeding cows and hauling hay, and I was stuck inside helping Mama clean house. Cindy, my older sister, was in charge of bossing us around.

Finally, when we had finished Mama's long list of chores, I was excited for a nice afternoon of horseback riding. As I was getting ready to head out, I heard Mama shout, "Don't be too long. You've got apple picking to do before it gets dark!" Me, trying to be clever, said, "Mama, I better take my horse 'cause I'm not tall enough to reach the apples." Being a mother of four, she wasn't easily outwitted, and she quickly responded, "I will bring the ladder. No need for that old horse of yours to eat more apples than we can pick."

I headed out the back door and toward the lot where I could climb up ol' Champ, our strawberry-roan horse. Daddy always told us, "You're lucky in life if you get one good dog, one good horse, and one good woman. And you better treat them all with respect or they'll leave you." Champ was that good horse. He was kid-proof, a good companion, and loved our summer outings.

As I was riding out of the driveway, I noticed a burlap bag on the fence. And then a brilliant idea came to me. It would be a time-saver and Mama would be so proud if, when I came back from my ride, I had already picked apples for her. So from our house I rode west and a little north to where the fruit trees were abundant with a variety of peaches, apples, and apricots. It was like the Garden of Eden. Well, almost. More like the gardens in town. You see, I knew of all the fruit hot spots in town by going down the alleyways. Town folks had great fruit trees because they were fertilized and watered regularly. Those alleyways were like a fruit picker's paradise. Did I have permission? Well, not exactly, but I did have a strict code of ethics I abided by. I only grabbed the fruit that was dangling over the fence line into the alley, which to me seemed like fair game.

My first stop was Dorothy Street and the plump, ripe apricots. Champ was my taste tester, and if he approved, I would go to picking and filling the sack. I got my sack a quarter of the way full, and it was time to move on. About two blocks north, I had arrived at Mrs. Pierce's house and her apple trees. Now, I didn't really know her, but she had a reputation from the kids at school to be a little scary and mean. My oldest brother always told me not to let her catch me snooping around her place. So I told Champ we must be in sneak mode! No nickering, no extra fruit picking, and to stay still. But who was I kidding? Apples were his weakness, and mine too, because I knew Mama was going to use them to make caramel apple pie.

However, I had a plan for this picking palooza. I backed Champ up to the apple tree and held the reins in my mouth to hold him still. That way his head was away from the tree and he couldn't start munching down and making a bunch of noise. Then it was like I was participating in the Olympic sport of apple picking! My hands were going as fast as they could go, apple by apple. About the time I was really getting into my groove, I heard the screen door slam in Mrs. Pierce's backyard, a dog bark, and the familiar sound of a Red Ryder BB gun going off. Between the slats of the fence, I could make out that gun being pointed right at us. Champ had already been fidgeting due to the no-pretasting policy, but when a BB hit him in the butt . . . Houston, we have a problem, 'cause I went into orbit.

I landed in her backyard, and Champ, with the sack of fruit, was already halfway home before I hit the ground. Much to Mrs. Pierce's surprise, what she thought was a crow in her fruit tree was actually a little cowboy.

As with many of the conversations Mama had on her kids' behalf and defense, I never knew all the details of the talk between her and Mrs. Pierce. However, I do remember picking, peeling, and sacking a lot of fruit for Mrs. Pierce that summer. Folks, all I can tell you for sure is, it is a whole lot safer to pick an apple from the store than it is in the wild alleys of town.

"It is a whole lot safer to pick an apple from the store than it is in the wild alleys of town."

If you haven't tried this dish before, you are missing out. This sets up like a firm pudding, with a rich caramel and vanilla flavor. We also add a splash of bourbon to balance out some of the sweetness. Reserve some of the caramel sauce to cool, then break it into small pieces for a little crunch on the top.

CARAMEL CRUNCH FLAN

MAKES 4 SERVINGS

PREP TIME: 10 MINUTES

TOTAL TIME: 55 MINUTES

Butter, for greasing

1 (14-ounce) can sweetened condensed milk

½ (12-ounce) can evaporated milk

1 cup heavy cream, at room temperature

3 large eggs, at room temperature

1 tablespoon vanilla extract

1 teaspoon ground cinnamon

1 cup sugar

1 tablespoon whiskey or bourbon

Boiling water, for the baking dish

1. Position a rack in the middle of the oven and preheat the oven to 350°F. Lightly butter four ramekins and set aside.

2. In a large bowl, whisk together the condensed milk, evaporated milk, cream, eggs, vanilla, and cinnamon until smooth.

3. Place the sugar in a nonstick skillet over medium heat. Stir with a rubber spatula to prevent burning until it becomes a smooth caramel, about 4 minutes.

4. Stir in the whiskey or bourbon and continue cooking 1 to 2 minutes, stirring constantly.

5. Evenly divide the sauce among the prepared ramekins, reserving about 3 tablespoons. Pour the reserved sauce onto parchment paper and set aside to cool.

6. Lightly stir the milk mixture and evenly divide among the ramekins. Place the ramekins into a large casserole dish. Pour boiling water into the dish until it reaches about two-thirds up the side of the ramekins.

7. Place the dish in the oven and bake for about 45 minutes, or until an inserted toothpick comes out clean.

8. Remove the casserole dish from the oven, and leave the ramekins in the water for 10 to 15 minutes. Remove the ramekins from the water and let cool to room temperature. Place the ramekins in the fridge and chill for at least 2 hours. As the flan chills, it will slightly change in consistency. A 2-hour chill creates a softer flan, while a 4-hour chill will create more of a cheesecake consistency.

9. When ready to serve, score the outside edges of the ramekins and invert on a plate. Break the cooled reserved sauce into pieces and sprinkle evenly on top of the flan. Serve.

This classic cake is buttery with a caramelized brown sugar topping. When you flip the cake over, the juices seep down and give it more moisture and flavor. The pineapple and cherries add a colorful presentation and fruity flavor that you can serve year-round.

PINEAPPLE UPSIDE-DOWN CAKE

MAKES ONE 9-INCH CAKE

PREP TIME: 10 MINUTES

TOTAL TIME: 1 HOUR AND 10 MINUTES

4 tablespoons butter, melted

$\frac{1}{2}$ cup packed light brown sugar

1 (15-ounce) can pineapple slices, $1\frac{1}{2}$ tablespoons juice reserved

7 maraschino cherries, $1\frac{1}{2}$ tablespoons juice reserved

1 teaspoon almond extract

$1\frac{1}{2}$ cups sifted all-purpose flour

2 teaspoons baking powder

$\frac{1}{2}$ teaspoon salt

$\frac{1}{3}$ cup shortening

$\frac{2}{3}$ cup granulated sugar

$\frac{2}{3}$ cup milk

1 large egg

1 teaspoon vanilla extract

1. Position a rack in the middle of the oven and preheat the oven to 350°F.

2. Pour the butter into a 9-inch cake pan and swirl around to evenly coat the bottom and walls. Sprinkle the brown sugar in the bottom of the pan and lightly mash around with a spatula to create a crust.

3. Place the pineapple rings in an even layer on top of the brown sugar.

4. In a small bowl, combine the cherries and almond extract. Place the cherries in the center holes of the pineapples.

5. In a large bowl, combine the flour, baking powder, and salt.

6. In another large bowl, stir together the shortening and granulated sugar until the mixture is crumbly. Whisk in the milk, egg, and vanilla until smooth.

7. Slowly stir the wet mixture into the flour mixture with a spoon. Be careful not to overstir. Spread the cake batter evenly on top of the pineapples.

8. Bake for 30 to 40 minutes, until an inserted toothpick comes out clean.

9. Meanwhile, in a small bowl, mix together the reserved pineapple juice and cherry juice. When the cake is done baking, poke several holes in the cake and pour the juice mixture evenly on top. Let the cake rest for 20 minutes.

10. Score the outside edge of the cake and invert on a plate. Cut and serve.

This is a classic dessert at every Mexican restaurant and something we always look forward to. It's a treat of fried dough that can be served sweet or savory. The trick to getting sopapillas to puff up the best is to spoon some of the hot oil up on the top of the dough as it fries. These can be filled with meat or vegetables like a meat pie, or just pour some honey on top and sprinkle with powdered sugar for a sweet treat.

SOPAPILLAS

MAKES ABOUT 12 SOPAPILLAS

PREP TIME: 25 MINUTES
TOTAL TIME: 35 MINUTES

2 cups all-purpose flour, plus more for dusting

1 tablespoon baking powder

1 teaspoon salt

2 tablespoons lard or shortening

Oil, for frying

Butter, honey, and/or powdered sugar, for serving (optional)

1. In a large bowl, combine the flour, baking powder, and salt. Cut in the lard with a spoon or fork until there are no large pieces.

2. Slowly stir in ¾ cup warm water until a soft ball forms. With your hands, knead the dough for 4 to 5 minutes. Cover with a towel and let rest for 20 minutes.

3. Meanwhile, in a large saucepan or Dutch oven, heat about 3 inches of oil to 370°F.

4. Roll the dough out onto a floured surface to about ⅛ inch thick. Cut the dough into about twelve 3 × 3-inch squares.

5. Working in batches, carefully add the sopapillas, a few at a time, to the hot oil. When they float and slightly begin to puff up, carefully spoon some oil up on top. Continue spooning oil until they puff up and turn a light golden brown, 2 to 3 minutes. Remove with a slotted spoon and transfer to a wire rack or paper towels to cool slightly and drain. Serve warm with butter, honey, and/or powdered sugar, if desired.

TIP You can flip the squares over while frying, but they puff up better when you spoon oil on top.

What is a more iconic Dutch oven dish than a cobbler? If you haven't tried it, we encourage you to give this a shot in the great outdoors. If you have ever picked fresh blackberries, then you know those vines have a lot of thorns, but the scratches are worth the trouble to make this easy dessert. The batter cooks up and over the berries for a perfect mix of a pudding and cake consistency. Brown sugar sprinkled on top while it bakes makes a light crust. As we say, "Get you some 'nillar ice cream and get after it!"

BLACKBERRY COBBLER

MAKES ABOUT 8 SERVINGS

PREP TIME: 10 MINUTES

TOTAL TIME: 1 HOUR AND 10 MINUTES

Butter, for greasing

2 cups granulated sugar

2 cups all-purpose flour

4 teaspoons baking powder

1 teaspoon ground cinnamon

1 teaspoon salt

1¾ cups milk

1 stick butter, melted

4 cups fresh or frozen blackberries (see Tip)

4 tablespoons light brown sugar

1. Position a rack in the middle of the oven and preheat the oven to 350°F. Butter an 11 × 13-inch pan or 12-inch Dutch oven and set aside.

2. In a large bowl, mix together the granulated sugar, flour, baking powder, cinnamon, and salt.

3. Whisk in the milk and melted butter until smooth. Pour the batter into the prepared pan.

4. Evenly top the batter with the blackberries.

5. Bake for about 50 minutes. Remove from the oven and sprinkle with the brown sugar. Continue to bake for about 10 minutes, or until golden brown and set to your desired consistency. Let cool slightly before serving to allow the cobbler to set up a bit.

TIP If using frozen blackberries, allow the berries to thaw, then pat dry with paper towels before adding to the batter.

THE ROUND PEN

If you have been in the business of breaking or starting two-year-old colts, then you have heard someone refer to the round pen. It was usually a sturdy, circular pen that was bullet-proof . . . and bronc-proof.

Back in my day, you would snub a broncy colt up to a stout horse, mount up, and see how long you could hang on. This may sound a little extreme, but I can tell you from experience, it's a whole lot safer in the round pen than Daddy's old-fashioned *on method*. It was very simple—you got on and you hung on for dear life. I think the old cowboys who gathered around the outsides of the pen really liked to see how high a colt might be able to launch a kid into orbit. Sunday afternoons in the round pen were either a form of torture or entertainment.

The typical round pen was a trotted, packed, round circle about eighty feet in diameter. The outside barrier was made of cedar staves woven into the fence. This pen was where school began. Classes started early and sometimes went overtime without recess. Repetition of trotting in circles, first with the horse unsaddled, then eventually saddled. A long set of lead lines and a hackamore* was all the control you had.

Groundwork was put in day after day, going in circles over and over.

Horses are naturally herd animals, and when you take a horse away from the herd, he feels vulnerable. The goal is to build trust. Isn't it amazing that the same thing happens to us when we get in new situations and surroundings? We don't like to feel isolated, so we go back to what we trust. My brother Randy, who was one of the best horse trainers I have ever known, would say, "It takes a lot of wet saddle blankets to make a colt into a horse you can trust. Just like it takes repetition, determination, and hard work to become a man that folks can trust."

That old round pen taught us a whole bunch about horses and twice as much about life. Life is a series of lessons, and sometimes they need to be repeated over and over to sink in, but the important ones usually do. Daddy would remind us, "Learn from your surroundings and change to fit them." There are uncomfortable moments in life when you are away from the familiar, but it's about learning how to saddle up and ride the new road you're on. I can also nearly guarantee you that the longer you sit in that saddle, the more comfortable you'll become.

* *Hackamore:* a halter without a bit, with a rawhide strap that fits across the horse's nose.

Shannon requested I create one of her favorite desserts because she loves the cinnamon and sugar crispy outside and soft inside. I decided to make this dessert a little more "adult" by creating a dipping sauce mixed with coffee and whiskey, which gives the sugary base of these churros a nice balance.

CHURROS WITH CARAMEL COFFEE SAUCE

MAKES 15 TO 20 CHURROS

PREP TIME: 10 MINUTES
TOTAL TIME: 25 MINUTES

½ cup plus 3 tablespoons granulated sugar

2 tablespoons ground cinnamon

2 cinnamon sticks

4 tablespoons butter

1 teaspoon vanilla extract

2 cups sifted all-purpose flour, plus ½ cup more as needed

3 tablespoons sifted brown sugar

2 teaspoons baking powder

1 teaspoon salt

2 large eggs, beaten

Oil, for frying

Caramel Coffee Sauce (recipe follows)

1. In a shallow bowl, combine ½ cup of the granulated sugar and the cinnamon. Set aside.

2. Place the cinnamon sticks in a large saucepan or pot and add 2 cups water. Bring to a boil over high heat for 2 to 3 minutes.

3. Remove the cinnamon sticks and reduce the heat to low. Stir in the butter and vanilla. Continue stirring until the butter has melted.

4. In a medium bowl, combine 2 cups of the flour, the remaining 3 tablespoons granulated sugar, the brown sugar, baking powder, and salt. Slowly stir the flour mixture into the cinnamon water. When the flour has been absorbed, remove the pan from the heat. Stir in the eggs. Add more flour if needed to get a thick cookie dough consistency.

5. Place the dough into a piping bag with a large open-star piping nozzle attached.

6. In a large saucepan or Dutch oven, heat 2 to 3 inches of oil to 350°F.

7. Pipe the dough into the oil in about 8-inch strands. Fry until a light golden brown, rotating as needed, 2 to 3 minutes.

8. Strain the churros from the oil and immediately toss in the cinnamon sugar mixture to generously coat. Transfer to a wire rack to cool slightly. Serve warm with the caramel coffee sauce.

CARAMEL COFFEE SAUCE

MAKES ABOUT ¾ CUP

PREP TIME: 10 MINUTES

TOTAL TIME: 25 MINUTES

4 tablespoons butter

½ cup granulated sugar

½ cup packed light brown sugar

¼ cup evaporated milk

1 tablespoon instant coffee

1 tablespoon whiskey or bourbon

1 teaspoon vanilla extract

1. In a small saucepan over medium heat, melt the butter. Stir in the granulated sugar and brown sugar until combined. Stir in the evaporated milk, instant coffee, and whiskey. Bring to a boil for 2 to 3 minutes, stirring frequently.

2. Remove from the heat and whisk in the vanilla. Let cool to room temperature and serve with churros.

This is an all-American classic apple pie with a homemade salted caramel sauce. To give it the perfect flavor, we are combining sweet apples, like Fuji, Gala, or Honeycrisp, with tart Granny Smiths. I recommend baking in a deep pie dish because this is going to be a heaping mound of goodness.

CARAMEL APPLE PIE

MAKES ONE 9-INCH PIE

PREP TIME: 15 MINUTES

TOTAL TIME: 3 HOURS AND 5 MINUTES

Sauce

1 stick butter

¾ cup heavy cream

¼ cup granulated sugar

¼ cup packed light brown sugar

3 teaspoons cornstarch

1 teaspoon vanilla extract

½ to 1 tablespoon coarse sea salt

Filling

3 Granny Smith apples, peeled and cored

3 sweet apples, such as Fuji, Gala, or Honeycrisp, peeled and cored

½ cup granulated sugar

½ cup packed light brown sugar

⅓ cup all-purpose flour

1 tablespoon cornstarch

2 teaspoons ground cinnamon

1 tablespoon lemon juice

2 store-bought prerolled pie crusts, or Best Flaky Pie Crust (page 242), rolled out and unbaked

1 large egg

1. Position a rack in the middle of the oven and preheat the oven to 375°F.

2. Make the sauce: In a small saucepan over medium-low heat, melt the butter. Whisk in the cream, granulated sugar, and brown sugar until smooth. Bring to a boil.

3. In a small bowl, whisk together the cornstarch and ¼ cup water. Stir into the cream mixture and cook, stirring constantly, until the mixture thickens, 2 to 3 minutes.

4. Remove from the heat and stir in the vanilla and the sea salt to taste. Set aside.

5. Make the filling: Thinly slice the apples and place them in a large bowl.

6. In a small bowl, combine the granulated sugar, brown sugar, flour, cornstarch, and cinnamon. Sprinkle over the apples and toss to coat well.

7. Sprinkle the lemon juice over the tops of the apples.

8. Place 1 pie crust in the bottom of a deep 9-inch pie plate.

9. Spread the apples evenly over the crust. Drizzle about ½ cup of the caramel sauce over the apples. Top with the remaining crust and cut six vent holes.

10. In a small bowl, whisk together the egg and 1 tablespoon water. Brush over the top of the crust.

11. Bake for about 50 minutes, or until the crust sets up and the pie is bubbling throughout. You may need to use a pie shield around the outside edges as it cooks to prevent it from burning.

12. Remove from the oven and let rest for at least 2 hours to let the pie set up. Slice and drizzle with the remaining caramel sauce before serving.

I know the filling of the pie is important, but I think what really makes a pie good and memorable is the crust. I always judge the goodness of a crust by how many flaky layers you can count . . . and this one has a bunch. Be sure the butter and lard are chilled well so the fat will better incorporate into the dough. A little vinegar gives this crust extra flaky layers.

BEST FLAKY PIE CRUST

MAKES TWO 9-INCH PIE CRUSTS

PREP TIME: 10 MINUTES
TOTAL TIME: 2 HOURS AND 45 MINUTES

2½ cups all-purpose flour, plus more for dusting

3 teaspoons baking powder

1 teaspoon salt

1 teaspoon ground cinnamon (optional)

6 tablespoons chilled butter

¾ cup chilled lard or shortening

¼ cup ice water

¼ cup apple cider vinegar

1. In a large bowl, combine the flour, baking powder, salt, and, if using, cinnamon. Slice or grate the butter and shortening into the mix.

2. With a pastry cutter or fork, cut the butter and shortening into the flour mixture, until it becomes a cracker crumb consistency but still has some butter and shortening chunks in it.

3. Fold in the ice water, a tablespoon at a time. Stir in the vinegar.

4. Flour your hands and begin working the dough into a ball. Place the dough on a floured surface and cut it into 2 equal pieces. Wrap the dough in plastic wrap and place in the fridge for at least 2 hours to chill.

5. When ready to use, preheat the oven to 375°F. Roll the dough out to about ⅛ inch thick.

6. To blind bake, place the dough in a 9-inch pie pan. Line the bottom with parchment paper and fill with dry beans or pie weights. Bake for 15 minutes. Remove the beans and parchment paper and return the pie to the oven. Bake an additional 10 to 15 minutes, or until a light golden brown and set.

TIP This dough can be frozen until ready to use. Let the dough thaw before baking and using in recipes.

This was a recipe title we never could understand as kids. But, according to Mama, we all acted like a bunch of monkeys after we had a double helping! I have changed this recipe up since my childhood, adding caramel and pecan turtles inside every dough ball for a gooey treat. However, you could change it up and add your favorite candy bar bits. Long ago, these were also called Millionaires, hence the name of this recipe. This is a great dessert, but you can also enjoy it at breakfast with a good cup of cowboy coffee.

MILLION-DOLLAR MONKEY BREAD

MAKES ABOUT 15 SERVINGS

PREP TIME: 15 MINUTES

TOTAL TIME: 1 HOUR AND 5 MINUTES

2 sticks butter, plus more for greasing

½ cup packed light brown sugar

1 tablespoon ground cinnamon

¾ cup granulated sugar

¼ cup cocoa powder

3 cans (8-count each) biscuits

24 pieces turtle candies, halved

½ cup chopped pecans

1. Position a rack in the middle of the oven and preheat the oven to 350°F. Butter a Bundt pan and set aside.

2. In a medium saucepan over medium heat, melt the butter. Whisk in the brown sugar and cinnamon. Continue cooking, stirring frequently, until the sauce thickens, about 4 minutes.

3. In small bowl, combine the granulated sugar and cocoa powder.

4. Cut the biscuits in half. Fold each half biscuit around a half piece of turtle candy. Roll around in your hand to form a ball.

5. Roll each ball into the sugar and cocoa mixture to generously coat. Begin layering the dough balls in the prepared Bundt pan. After using about half of the ingredients, pour half of the brown sugar sauce over the top of the dish. Evenly sprinkle half of the pecans on top. Continue layering the dough balls until all have been used. Top with the remaining caramel sauce and pecans.

6. Bake for 40 to 50 minutes, until golden brown on top. Let cool for about 5 minutes. Place a plate over the Bundt pan and invert to release the bread. Serve warm.

NATURE'S WEATHER SIGNS

When pouring a cup of coffee, if the bubbles move to the outside, fair weather is ahead. If the bubbles move to the middle, a storm is coming.

Slice open a persimmon seed. If it looks like a spoon, it means a snowy winter; if it looks like a fork, it will be a mild winter; if it is shaped like a knife, expect a cold winter.

A wasp's nest found low to the ground means an early frost and possible bad winter.

Branding iron smoke or chimney smoke that falls downward and stays close to the ground means a storm is coming.

When ants are lazy and sluggish, a storm is coming. Before a hard rain, they will also build higher mounds to prevent rainwater from coming in.

Birds tend to fly lower to the ground when a storm is approaching.

Spiders often abandon their webs and move onto tent or camp walls when bad weather is coming.

A halo around the moon may be signaling the approach of a warm front and possible precipitation.

Red sky at night, sailor's delight. Red sky in the morning, sailor's warning. A red or pink sunset means fair weather, because skies are clear and most weather comes from the west. The color is caused by dust.

When roosters crow later in the day, it's going to rain.

Bees busy late in the summer means a hard winter ahead.

The thicker the coat on a woolly bear caterpillar, the colder the winter. If there is a wide brown band between two black bands, the winter won't be so bad. If it doesn't have a brown band, the winter will be severe.

There are few things that are better to me than the smell of cookies baking in the oven . . . especially if they are peanut butter cookies. I do have an issue with this type of cookie, however, because a lot of times they can be hard and brittle when you bite into one. Not these! They will stay soft, which is the best way to serve them. Just be sure not to overbake them, which can cause them to harden as they cool.

SOFT PEANUT BUTTER COOKIES

MAKES ABOUT 24 COOKIES

PREP TIME: 15 MINUTES
TOTAL TIME: 30 MINUTES

2 sticks unsalted butter, softened
1 cup packed light brown sugar

¾ cup granulated sugar, plus more for sprinkling
2 large eggs
1 cup creamy peanut butter

1 teaspoon vanilla extract
2½ cups all-purpose flour
2 teaspoons baking soda

1. Position a rack in the middle of the oven and preheat the oven to 350°F. Line a baking sheet with parchment paper and set aside.

2. In a medium bowl, cream together the butter, brown sugar, and granulated sugar.

3. In a large bowl, whisk together the eggs, peanut butter, and vanilla until smooth.

4. Sift in the flour and baking soda.

5. Pinch off about 24 golf ball–size balls. Place on the prepared baking sheet and flatten each ball slightly with a fork in a crisscross pattern. Sprinkle the top of each cookie with a little granulated sugar.

6. Bake for 10 to 12 minutes. Be careful not to overbake, as they will set up a little as they cool. Remove from the oven and place on a wire rack to cool. Serve warm or at room temperature.

"If you've never been bucked off, then you ain't be riding long enough."

This is my most favorite brownie ever. It was originally inspired by my all-time favorite TV dinner, the Hungry-Man Salisbury Steak. Like any good dessert recipe, butter is the key ingredient here. This brownie also has a rich chocolate taste that isn't too overpowering. And if you're like me, don't be afraid to serve these hot out of the oven with an extra pat of butter on top.

DECADENT BUTTER BROWNIE

MAKES 12 BROWNIES

PREP TIME: 5 MINUTES
TOTAL TIME: 35 MINUTES

Butter, for greasing
2 cups sugar

1½ cups all-purpose flour
½ cup cocoa powder
1 teaspoon baking powder
1 teaspoon ground cinnamon

½ teaspoon salt
4 large eggs, beaten
2 sticks butter, melted

1. Position a rack in the middle of the oven and preheat the oven to 350°F. Butter a 9 × 13-inch baking pan and set aside.

2. In a large bowl, combine the sugar, flour, cocoa powder, baking powder, cinnamon, and salt. Whisk in the eggs and melted butter.

3. Pour the batter into the prepared pan. Bake for 25 to 30 minutes, until an inserted toothpick comes out clean. Let cool slightly or to room temperature before cutting and serving.

This recipe comes from Mama, who made these bars all the time for the grandkids. I think they loved them so much because they taste a lot like their favorite cereal, Cinnamon Toast Crunch. These are soft and slightly gooey bars with a cinnamon, sugar, and honey base. Top it off with a simple powdered sugar glaze mixed with a little mayonnaise to give it a tang.

HONEY CINNAMON BARS

MAKES 16 BARS

PREP TIME: 5 MINUTES
TOTAL TIME: 20 MINUTES

Butter, for greasing
1½ sticks butter, melted
¾ cup granulated sugar

¼ cup packed light brown sugar
¼ cup honey
1 large egg
1 teaspoon baking soda
1 teaspoon ground cinnamon

¼ teaspoon salt
2 cups all-purpose flour
1½ cups powdered sugar
2 tablespoons mayonnaise
2 teaspoons vanilla extract

1. Position a rack in the middle of the oven and preheat the oven to 350°F. Butter an 11 × 15-inch baking pan.

2. In a large bowl, using an electric mixer on high speed, beat together the melted butter, granulated sugar, brown sugar, honey, and egg until smooth. Beat in the baking soda, cinnamon, and salt. Slowly beat in the flour until combined.

3. Spread the mixture into the baking pan. Bake for 10 to 15 minutes, until a light golden brown on top and puffed up along the edges. The bars will be soft and spongy but will set up as they cool. Place on a wire rack to cool.

4. Meanwhile, in a small bowl, whisk together the powdered sugar, mayonnaise, vanilla, and 1 to 2 tablespoons water, or until a spreadable consistency. Spread over the warm bars. Allow the bars to cool completely, cut, and serve.

This is not like your traditional coconut cream pie, and that's the way I like it! Instead of using the traditional canned coconut milk, we're using regular coconut milk, which will give a more mellow coconut flavor that isn't overpowering. We're also topping this with a whipping cream instead of meringue because I like a denser, sweetened topper for a pie. Finish this off with some toasted coconut flakes for what Shan calls "presentation."

COCONUT CREAM PIE

MAKES ONE 9-INCH PIE

PREP TIME: 10 MINUTES

TOTAL TIME: 1 HOUR AND 50 MINUTES

1½ cups flaked sweetened coconut

1½ cups sweetened coconut milk (not from a can)

2½ cups heavy cream

5 large egg yolks

1 cup sugar

5 tablespoons cornstarch

1 tablespoon butter

½ teaspoon salt

2 teaspoons vanilla extract

1 prebaked 9-inch store-bought prepared pie crust, or ½ recipe Best Flaky Pie Crust (page 242), blind baked in a 9-inch pie pan

1. Position a rack in the middle of the oven and preheat the oven to 350°F.

2. Scatter ½ cup of the coconut flakes in a small baking pan. Bake for 8 to 10 minutes, until the flakes are lightly toasted.

3. Meanwhile, whisk together the coconut milk, 1¼ cups of the cream, and the egg yolks.

4. In a medium saucepan over medium-low heat, whisk together ¾ cup of the sugar and the cornstarch. Slowly whisk in the egg mixture.

5. Bring the mixture to a boil, whisking constantly for 1 minute.

6. Remove the pan from the heat and whisk in the butter, salt, the remaining 1 cup coconut flakes, and the vanilla. Scrape the filling into the pie crust. Let cool about 10 minutes, then cover and place in the fridge for 1½ hours to completely chill.

7. Meanwhile, in a medium bowl, using an electric mixer on high speed, beat the remaining 1¼ cups cream with the remaining ¼ cup sugar until stiff. Evenly spread the whipped cream on top of the chilled pie. Top with toasted coconut flakes and serve chilled.

INDEX

Note: Page references in *italics* indicate photographs.